Solastalgia

FOUR PALACES
—— PUBLISHING ——

Copyright ©2025 by Four Palaces Publishing

All rights reserved

ISBN: 979-8-218-61677-9

Cover art by Lydia Yost
Book design by Emily Townsend

Four Palaces Publishing
Dallas, TX
https://fourpalaces.org/

Contents

Introduction   vii

A Matter of Tide   1
MARIE WINFIELD

The Deep Blue Between   7
KYRA MATHEWS

When a Man Tricked a Brook   15
CAROLYN JONES

A Tidal Triptych   26
R. D. SALMON

**Water, Land, People -
The Price of Progress**   33
MONISHA RAMAN

The Memory of Calmer Seas   44
CAITLIN CACCIATORE

CONTENTS

Fire Hardening — 52
CLAIRE ROBERTSON-PREIS

Chased From Home — 60
JO MORGAN SLOAN

Beauty in the Burn Scar — 68
REBEKAH DOYLE

The Atmosphere Between Us — 76
ISAAC PEARLMAN

The New-Moon Bird — 84
EILEEN MCLELLAN

My First Love, an Orange Spring — 90
ALLISON BARNETT

No Going Home Anymore — 96
LAURA SELDNER

About the Contributors — 109

About the Guest Judge — 113

Introduction

NOSTALGIA IS HARDWIRED into our brain chemistry. It is a familiar, complicated emotion, tied to our relationship with memory and identity; a way to consciously cope with the passage of time. Solastalgia, though not technically a form of nostalgia by strict definition, feels awfully similar: a double helix of joy and melancholy felt when retrieving a specific memory. Narrowing this feeling further, solastalgia pinpoints the nostalgic target of *home*. It is that same nostalgic longing, but for a physical place—a sort of homesickness for something long lost to time. What differentiates the experience of solastalgia from classic nostalgia, is that we are feeling that melancholic memory retrieval of home as the loss of it is actually happening. Not what has *been lost*, but what we are *actively losing*. While we exist in this place—right here, right now—we are engaging in the acute, catastrophic self-awareness.

There is a reason that post-apocalyptic scenes feature the same, harrowing landscape: the infrastructure humans built, over time, taken over by the Earth. An abandoned childhood home, left to the goodwill of time on this planet will collapse into soil, overtaken by growth and wildness. It is an innate fear humanity shares—a grave understanding that all we have built as a society is in direct opposition to the natural world. The particular distress of solastalgia is therefore further defined by identifying environmental changes as the direct cause for our loss of home and place. It is not as simple as feeling homesick; it is recognizing the specific impact of external factors that are erasing our homes in real time from under our (naïvely) firmly planted feet.

It is natural to long for a specific place-time, to mourn and grieve our past selves and the places we have called home throughout our lives, places that feature in memory and identity as we, too, suffer the inescapable march of time. What is unnatural to this process is the exacerbated speed and reasonings by which we are losing those places. It is not just to time. It is to climate change, gentrification, and overdevelopment working together in bludgeoning erasure. This is a difficult reality to accept, one that manifests in phrases like *climate anxiety* and *urban displacement*. We know for a fact that not only displacement caused by climate change, but also gentrification and overdevelopment, cause significant psychological distress. This is not a new concept; settler-colonialism, Manifest Destiny, and white supremacy have long patented destruction and erasure of entire places, cultures, and homes. In late-stage capitalism, with hyper-paced greed and its consequences at the helm of Earth's fate, though our most vulnerable communities face this destruction most adamantly, we are all at risk.

Through the following writings, authors do not simply wallow in despair and melancholic longing; they identify root causes of experiencing the phenomenon of solastalgia while inviting the reader into a shared memory. A united community tied down by immense grief, but as resilient as the Earth herself, memories are retrieved, and futures are written—despite all the damage we've done as a species. These are, in their truest form, writings of hope.

There are three sections in this collection of thirteen essays. Essays relay the experience of solastalgia within these categories, determined through basic elements of matter: *Water, Fire,* and *Ecosphere*. These sections are categorized by not how these elements act as a theme tying essays together, but as a sensory trigger for our own memories and how we contextualize these dramatic changes to our planet within our own lived realities.

The first section, *Water*, speaks to an ever-present entity, all powerful and all-changing. Unlike on solid ground, upon which we build our cities and lives and farms and roads, water is mutable. It is a vessel of continuous change—and therefore, a delicate lesson in balance. If you do not relax and allow the ocean to carry you, you'll thrash and fight until you drown. You have to let go; let the water take you. As these essays explore solastalgia through the writers' relationships with water, we learn how to negotiate our existence under its tender authority.

In "Water, Land, People: The Price of Progress" by Monisha Raman, flashes of lyrical prose weave together the elements of *water*, *land*, and *people* to relay the consequence of developing the natural world in the name of human progress. "The lake, tranquil in its stillness, lays calm as the wind draws ripples on its surface, constantly flowing as if seeking something beyond its barriers," she lovingly describes of her home of Chennai, a coastal city in India. Thalumber Lake, the center of life within this landscape, has undergone many changes in the centuries it has existed alongside its people. But can it survive the existential threat of modern humanity?

Carolyn Jones attempts to answer a similar inquiry in her essay "When a Man Tricked a Brook," as she critically analyzes the political history of human development and our attempt to control nature, posture as ruler over something as uncontainable as the element of water. Jones researches the history of floodwaters in her Princeton neighborhood, relaying the systemic disconnection between what we have built within our urban developments and what was sacrificed to do so. For Jones, it is an impossible mystery to solve as storms will worsen in the face of climate change and we reap the sins of decisions made far in the past—just as future generations will say of us.

Both "Tidal Triptych" by R. D. Salmon and "The Deep Blue Between" by Kyra Mathews explicitly explore the fragility of making a home near water. Salmon uses her love of beachcombing and amorous imagery to describe the temporality of the ocean and its tide, a deeper meaning revealed anecdotally when she relays, "Just a few hours ago, the sea was here, right here where I'm walking. Any and everything that was swimming or sloshing around in it ran the risk of getting left behind." Similarly, Mathews evokes lyrical prose to relive specific moments of her life by the sea, strung together as numbered memories to bring the reader into her special home place of Mumbai. It does not matter if we've visited Mumbai. Or Manhattan. Or Northern California. Or the Mountain West. We naturally are drawn to the comforts of water: "A friend tells me that when she stepped into the ocean for the first time in 5 years, it felt like coming home. A baptism, an awakening, an open door."

In "The Memory of Calmer Seas," Caitlin Cacciatore wants to know how, exactly, we can square the natural world with the dangerous, fragile one we have built, and the inequality of climate change's impacts. From her vantage point in Queens, "Hurricanes are not known for finding borders to be barriers to their destructive powers," as disaster is an outcome we must prepare for. And it is in Marie Winfield's winning essay "A Matter of Tide" that she does not only reminisce of all the things she will miss from her beloved New York, which will eventually find itself reclaimed by the sea—first due to governmental neglect, and then by imminent disaster—but actively attempts to notate those changes in order to salvage hope for her children's' future. She understands the dire consequences of inaction compounded impact of systemic racism in certain boroughs, from lack of federal funding to rezoning, a sort of double whammy of gentrification and climate change disaster all but signing the fate of residents. And yet, she makes clear that East Harlem "is my beloved place, layered and complicated, a palimpsest." There is no destruction that can outmatch the visceral, unwavering love of home.

Unlike water's representation of consistent change, fire symbolizes cleansing destruction. Fire is, especially if you grew up in the West, a deep-seated existential fear always lapping at your heels. In the second section of essays, *Fire*, the element takes, destroys. But fire also warms, provides, and cleanses. This fear-reverence dichotomy between the natural and unnatural is delicately and fiercely expressed in Rebekah Doyle's "Beauty in the Burn Scar." While she makes clear that "Fire is a part of the natural ecology of many landscapes in the Southwest," she must also face the increased sighting of burn scars as representation of accelerated climate change and a visceral reaction of "how this sadness extends to the children who will not know these places as I knew them in my lifetime."

Likewise, in "Fire Hardening," Claire Robertson-Preis studies the perversion of natural fire cycles and the human cause (and cost) of fire acceleration in the West, and how we must carve a path forward to salvage humanity's future. Despite the shared anxiety she expresses, Robertson-Preis so lovingly reminds us: "But for humanity, our creativity can help us find reasons to keep living in a world that needs saving." Jo Morgan Sloan echoes this sentimental acceptance of our new reality in "Chased From Home," as she relays a more personal account of surviving the threat of persistent wildfire seasons to her urban community, relaying, "With our go-bags pre-packed, our assets in photographs, and Nixle at the ready, one must admit a lonely homesickness for safe Mother Earth." We cannot help but agree with her when she plainly states: "No—I long for something that can't be repaired."

Finally, the collection ends with its third section, *Ecosphere*: an homage to the ways our planetary home sustains life, despite our present and future losses, in spite of our communal solastalgia. There is one central theme to the essays in this section: *we cannot go home*. This is poignantly expressed by Lauren Seldner in "No Going Home Anymore," in which she connects many personal memories to specific places, writing an homage to her identity and life experiences as she grieves a home that no longer exists. Perfectly capturing this universal feeling of attempting to revisit a physical place only to be met with loss, she writes that "Each time I returned, I only found a place that I recognized less and less." Regardless of the *why*, we all mourn our own distinct memories that function the same, because, "Every place I've ever walked is a graveyard where someone else's memories are buried."

In "The Atmosphere Between Us," climate scientist Isaac Pearlman presents hard truths of how the idea of *not going home anymore* has, and will continue to, impact specific global communities in ways that more privileged countries like the United States, despite our own profound losses, cannot fully comprehend on a mass scale. The existential threat that climate change poses to wipe certain areas quite literally off the map is unfathomable. "Would they care more," Pearlman asks, "if they heard how hard climate-fueled disasters have hit people across the world, and how it's a drop in the bucket compared to what lies ahead? If they knew the names and faces of those who stand to lose everything because of the United States' pollution and subsequent inaction?"

"New Moon Bird" wrestles with this inquiry, as Eileen McLellan investigates her relationship with her childhood home, a remote village in Wales, and its native avian species. This essay is a canary in the coal mine lesson intertwined with nostalgic tribute as she searches for her treasured curlew birds, only to find their absence representative of a greater, ecospheric loss. Witnessing the species flee these wetlands alongside the community fleeing economic collapse of the village, she too asks in an implied call to action: "What will we do when the last of our wild kin are gone and that pleasure lost?"

And finally, it is in "My First Love, An Orange Spring" that Allison Barnett connects sensory memory to solastalgia as she retrieves a memory of experiencing first love, its loss due to time, and the symbolic lesson of change, hope, and resilience that we can learn from the famous California perennial. "This is the thing about the California poppy," she presents to us, "it grows in the most inhospitable conditions, seeding itself as it pleases. It likes shallow, poorly watered soil. It likes to take root in impossibility, a stubborn wildflower that grows in the least expected places...You cannot tame it. You cannot make it yours. You just have to accept where it has decided to spring up and appreciate it where it has decided to grow."

Science tells us that each time we intentionally recall a memory, that act of retrieval fires up our neural pathways and renders the memory both stronger and resilient to disruption. Through sensory activation—a specific smell, the opening riff of a song, somatic touch of grass—can activate a stable memory, and if we close our eyes and let our senses and pathways navigate us, we are brought into a past moment like a strong dream. It is why sense of place—of home—can perforate the present with such an intense longing. It is through the sensory detail of place that these essays act as love letters to our rapidly changing reality in the midst of our homesickness, of ever-present loss. In the wake of displacement and erasure, these writers have immortalized and commemorated place and home so as not to forget. Every written word, every read sentence, a neural pathway ignites and defies permanent loss of what was.

If there is any lesson to be learned from the concept of solastalgia and the tragic reality from which it is birthed, it is that everything changes. In this framework, that change is not inherently good or evil, it is, like the unstoppable violent tide, the cleansing flames, simply *change*. While we cannot stop change—including the destruction we all face in some capacity by human hand—we *can* honor the past while fighting to build a softer, more resilient future. This is perhaps best captured by Winfield as she describes East Harlem as a place no life should grow, and yet, "life clearly went on, and goes on." But is it really that bleakly simple? Must we as a society face the fate of our cultural and physical landscape, do our best to hold onto our memories in the throngs of solastalgia? I believe Seldner answers this for all of us when she writes: "When I think of this town, I still remember it as it was and not as it is. And I want to think that places remember us, too. That the land recalls through its long and unfaltering memory the weight of those who set foot there. If it does, I hope it thinks of me kindly. I hope the land knows I found solace in every inch of forest, every field, every dirt path, every night under its blanket of stars. And I hope the land knows it was loved."

As you read this collection of essays compiled by the editors of Four

Palaces, Frederick Tran and Emily Townsend, I invite you to investigate the pinch of solastalgia you may also feel and what that means for your own resilience within a global community. Through essays about *Water, Fire, and Ecosphere*, we learn there are many ways to end. But these endings represent opportunity to begin, as well. Must we hold space for this longing, this homesickness, this grief, in order to hope and build and more than anything, remember as it once was?

Of course, we must. And we will.

WATER

A Matter of Tide

MARIE WINFIELD

THE SINKHOLES ON THE EAST RIVER ESPLANADE open up without warning, leaving nothing but air in between the walkway and the East River. I walked both of my daughters, first in strollers, then as wobbly toddlers, and later as strident kindergartners past the sinkholes year after year, wondering if one day we'd be swallowed up whole. I moved to East Harlem in 2010 before my first daughter turned 3 years old and my youngest followed not long after. Our route to the Esplanade took us from our front door on East 117th Street, where masses of people appeared in an exodus to the now-closed Target Superstore. From there, we turned down onto Pleasant Avenue, past the Love Café and infamous Rao's, which used to be known for gangsters and film stars more than the Mayor's post-election victory meal. We walked through Jefferson Park, where at any time of the day someone was setting up a BBQ and a birthday party and a soccer game. Past the dog run, up the ramp, across the FDR Drive and back down again and we were all of a sudden near the water, in a different universe. Fishermen cast their lines into the East River and waited patiently in their fold-up chairs. Joggers and bikers and power walkers made their way uptown and back downtown past the perennially fenced off pier at 107th Street. And I held my breath each time we passed a sinkhole, enclosing my daughters' small hands tighter in mine.

East Harlem is a paradoxical place to raise children, amid an official narrative that says no life should grow there. There is always someone explaining how we should not be, but life clearly went on and goes on. Every year, New York City publishes various studies with public health indicators showing how often our children need ER interventions for asthma, how the "heat island effect" plagues seniors during the summer months, how local playgrounds haven't been refurbished in decades. Sometimes, you'd notice groups touring the neighborhood: medical students being shown where the poor people they'd treat at the Mount Sinai clinic live, the next batch of Master's students at Columbia University visiting from the West Side to research how much worse things have gotten, or city planners doing site visits during a rezoning process. And yet every year, Italian families return to the neighborhood for the Giglio, flashing carnival lights and rides for kids on Pleasant Avenue, Puerto Rican flags wave up and down 116th Street, smiles spread from ear-to-ear at each NYCHA Family Day, somehow there's a camel in the cold of winter walking in the Three Kings Day parade through the streets of El Barrio. My oldest daughter would zoom past the sinkholes, paying them no mind, on her way to Randall's Island. We lived our lives anyway, as others treated this place we called home like a laboratory, an urban Truman Show set in Manhattan.

In *Lessons For Survival*, Emily Raboteau describes "solastalgia" as "the desolation caused by an assault on the beloved place where one resides; a feeling of dislocation one gets at home." Although she lived on the West side of Manhattan, and we on the East, the feelings were identical. That type of desolation's force of gravity pulls from all corners of the city, creating sinkholes in a collective faith that the places we call home will survive.

When I moved uptown, I felt like I was moving back "home" as if East Harlem was a part of NYC that couldn't be erased, a version of the city that matched my memories. It was where everyone wished me a Happy Mother's Day all day long in May, not necessarily because I had a kid but because it was a holiday, and mothers were second to Jesus. It was where in the summer people called my little girl Blondie because of the highlights in her hair and looked at her in the face and then at me and said *this is your daughter right?* instead of assuming I was the tall Black nanny, which would happen just 20 blocks downtown. It was the parades and festivals and NYCHA and barbecues but also shootings and the guy a couple of buildings down from me who stuffed a woman into a large suitcase and rolled it onto the street and left her with the regular trash pick-up. East Harlem was still its own place, not yet affected by the great Expansion uptown: the rezonings and new development, Citibanks and Citibikes and Starbucks, or the type of stores that closed up shop mad quick during the pandemic because the clientele all jumped ship for the Hamptons and Hudson Valley or wherever. East Harlem was still a credible location for *Law and Order* film shoots in Manhattan, but also now for blockbuster movies like *Annie* with Jamie Foxx and scenes on 116th Street with the then-Council Speaker's storefront office in the background. East Harlem is El Barrio and El Barrio is East Harlem. It is still the colorful murals and fishing off the Esplanade and syringes and soccer in the park and cuchifritos and community gardens that smelled like roasted pig. It is the Tito Puente statue that never got built and the pier at 107th Street cordoned off because at any moment it might wash away into the East River.

The East in East Harlem was important to me. I grew up off Second Avenue but downtown and came all the way up to the Upper East Side from kindergarten through twelfth grade to sit in a building with slits for windows and no ventilation before the days a novel virus reminded us that air might be important to our health. And my parents were still there on the East Side. They seemed like a lower East Side version of the Jeffersons, who made it into a building they never planned to leave. That could be said of everyone who won the Mitchell-Lama lottery, an affordable apartment to raise a family in Manhattan. Even if those residents did leave, they somehow never actually gave up those apartments. Who would? But I learned later that my father's attachment to this unnamed neighborhood was its proximity to Stuyvesant Town and Peter Cooper Village. He told a story at a local Black History Month event, explaining how as an uptown kid he came to visit his injured father who was recuperating at the Veterans' Hospital downtown. After one visit, my father came out of the hospital and noticed the leafy green complex across the way. He decided to take a look around and was promptly screamed at to get out, that he did not belong there. His place and his community work in this downtown neighborhood was a point of pride. I don't think he ever imagined being displaced from it.

When Hurricane Sandy hit, it came for the East Side.

My parents' neighborhood with no official name had no electricity either, leaving the traffic lights dark as they drove uptown. It took them about 100 blocks and a bit of luck to make it to East Harlem. My parents stayed in our bed, while we bunked with my eldest daughter. With no TV, my dad left the radio on what seemed like 24-7 for news updates. I wondered what would've happened if we hadn't moved back to NYC, where my parents would've gone, whether they would've stayed in the apartment downtown, in the dark, no fridge, no stove, no internet, no way to charge their phones. The research showed it could've very easily turned out the other way around, us trying to get downtown, no traffic lights, no FDR drive, an apocalyptic nightmare. If the tides had been different, if the hurricane had hit earlier, East Harlem would've been the area almost washed away.

City agencies knew this possibility. The City was well aware about those minutes and hours that saved East Harlem from Lower Manhattan's fate. This is why they requested a million dollars of federal, public money for consultants to figure out resiliency strategies for a neighborhood criss-crossed with hospital and NYCHA campuses, bodegas and high rises, playgrounds, parks and schools. The average income of East Harlem residents is low; local newspapers used to call our hood "Convict Alley," as it has one of the highest rates of people incarcerated at Rikers Island returning to the neighborhood. Another hour, higher tides and this population would have been those struggling the most.

Post-Sandy, Lower Manhattan got the Big-U, the plan to wall off lower Manhattan from the threat of rising sea levels. This meant a design competition, community meetings, copious amounts of funding, and the political will to make it happen. As I sat on my local Community Board uptown, we evaluated City projects and initiatives through the lens of the environment, open space and parks. Project after project came though the Board, as I waited for the recommendations of this resiliency report. Surely, if the City was committed to renovating the pier, creating a greenway and refurbishing the Esplanade, upgrading parks and playgrounds, it should be considering the recommendations that would come out of this comprehensive million dollar study. Right? The answers from City officials always sounded like the adults in *Peanuts*, a garbled mess of unintelligible sounds coming from somewhere underneath the East River.

The report took so long to finish that the neighborhood had already been rezoned, several Community Parks Initiative sites finished, and I'd left the committee that cared about such things. My youngest daughter was now well into elementary school but Zooming in due to the pandemic. My oldest daughter was in junior high school. The sinkholes loomed larger and more fencing kept small animals and children from falling into the East River. The recommendations in the report, though, were withheld from the community. We received the results of a Freedom of Information Law request for the consultants' findings: pages and pages of blacked out line after blacked out line, as if protecting our neighborhood from climate change required the same level of secrecy as operations out of Guantanamo Bay.

The repetition of those black lines contrasted with the white pages was the starkest moment of desolation. Each line was an attempt to erase this beloved place. Each black mark was a stroke of darkness denying the children that grow up in this neighborhood a bright future. Their future was underneath those lines. This 280-page report was a palimpsest, hiding the words that had the power to protect this community from the disastrous effects that missed us just because of the moon and the tides.

East Harlem is indeed my beloved place, where I chose to raise my children. On every street, there is evidence of something someone fought for: street co-namings of Black and Puerto Rican neighborhood legends, a school slated for closure still thriving, a reopened library, affordable housing, neglected and vacant plots of land turned into community gardens. There's a famous photo by Hiram Maristany of the Young Lords commandeering a City-operated tuberculosis truck in 1970. Artist Miguel Luciano brought back this image and others to the neighborhood in a public art installation called *Mapping Resistance: The Young Lords in El Barrio*. The words "Chest X-Ray Unit" are emblazoned on the back of the truck, as a group of about ten people are pushing the entire truck down a New York City street. They were effectively appropriating city funds and redistributing it to where the needs were highest: East Harlem. One of the images for the exhibit hung on the fences of a community garden, obscuring the fact that the garden would soon be shut down because of a larger development project. This is my beloved place, layered and complicated, a palimpsest.

It's not always easy to notice the change as you're living in it. As a mom, you notice the kids first: the marks on the wall showing how much they've grown, the too small clothes that go to Goodwill. And then it's: Didn't we used to wear winter coats for the school ice skating trip? Was it always this hot? when we trekked up the Morningside Park stairs to pick up the kids from summer camp. These long-limbed children of mine seemed to be trying to outgrow the pace at which the planet is simultaneously dying and trying to kill them. I wonder whether they will be fast enough to live a full life, the ones we'd dreamed for them, before those dreams are erased. Sometimes, it seems like that might only happen with a miracle.

If miracles exist and things go to plan, the crumbling pier on East 107th Street will now be rebuilt by 2027. My oldest daughter, who first push-kicked her way on her scooter past the sinkholes and then flew by the chain-linked pier on a bike, will be twenty years old then. I imagine her trying to make a meaningful life as she grows into a young woman, while simultaneously turning the tide. Because on this planet, that is what we are all now called to do.

The Deep Blue Between

KYRA MATHEWS

1. SEASHELLS, THE CASTAWAYS OF COUNTLESS TIDES, washed across my mother's bedside table. As a child, my mother told me that if you held the shells to your ear, you could hear the sound of the sea.

I used to tiptoe to her collection, and quickly grab one to my ear, convinced mermaids whispered inside, their secrets just out of reach. If only I was fast enough, I'd catch them mid-conversation. Minutes would melt into more minutes, standing still and concentrating with eyes closed and nose scrunched, hoping I'd hear the crash of a wave. I never did.

2. I have felt more at home submerged in or in close proximity to water than anywhere else classified as an "official" place of residence or nationality. The West Heights swimming pool. Kite Beach, Dubai. Kamari Beach, Santorini. Corniche Beach, Abu Dhabi (where I was also stung by a jellyfish). Prainha Beach Resort, Dona Paula, Goa (where I got married). Monterosso al Mare, Cinque Terre. Sant Sebastià Beach, Barcelona. Mon Repos Beach, Corfu. Karon Beach, Phuket.
It is where I sleep best. But in Mumbai, it is where I dreamt best.

3. Meticulously constructing Hokusai's The Great Wave off Kanagawa in LEGO, a mosaic of white and blue, I found myself an unwitting creator of tragedy. As the towering wave took shape, I noticed the tiny, headless LEGO figures, submerged in the crashing foam. A poignant reminder of the human cost often overlooked in grand artistic representations.

4. In recent years, I have avoided going back to Mumbai for many reasons. Traffic, pollution and too-rapid urbanization to start with. And while the construction of the Metro symbolizes the inevitable march of progress, it has also introduced the city to the felling of countless trees, the disruption of delicate ecosystems and contributed to the urban heat island effect. Simply put, it makes the city unrecognizable, and hard to breathe in.

The last time I went back, I found ghosts of myself, littered like flotsam on the sand. Unease lingered, a relentless mosquito buzz. I stayed for less than 24 hours, the familiar sea scent clinging to my skin like salt.

5. The city doesn't always hold its arms open or wait by the door with a drink ready at hand anymore. Maybe it's never forgiven me for leaving. Maybe I've never forgiven myself.

6. I store the sound of the sea in my bones, foam curling against my ribs, aching, whenever I board an aircraft that isn't homeward bound. For some, water is a hostile force, a threat to be overcome. For others, a source of life, a place of deep connection. Finality or renewal, drown or transform? Is it a metamorphosis or a homecoming? Do we undergo a fundamental change when entering water, or are we simply returning to something within us?

7. Oceans are cosmic cradles of complexity. From its tranquil surface to its abyssal depths, it is a realm of paradox, offering joy and sorrow, war and peace, strangeness and connection. Heraclitus built on this, and so did Nietzsche; it is impossible to overstate the creative power of oceans on our imagination and more importantly, on our origin story.

8. A friend tells me that when she stepped into the ocean for the first time in 5 years, it felt like coming home. A baptism, an awakening, an open door. She stayed in the water until she was a prune.

9. Shakespeare's plays are imbued with the potent symbolism of water. Its destructive force evident in the tempestuous seas that claim the lives of sailors and shatter Ophelia's sanity. Yet, water also serves as a catalyst for transformation. Viola, adrift on the currents of fate, emerges reborn.

Water's dual nature as both destroyer and renewer is pervasive, which explains why when I sometimes read his plays, I feel like I'm holding my breath.

10. At what age do you really know that love is love, and acknowledge it with pleasure like an old friend? The first time I knew love was love was for my hometown. Stranded in the rain with little money on us, my friends and I wandered around Bandra, Mumbai with a *vada pao* each, wrapped in newspaper, before continuing to explore the neighbourhood, infatuated, obsessed, giddy and feverish, damp cheeked and sweaty palmed, a key in my brain turning to hum, "so this is love" from *Cinderella*.

How lucky I was to have met it so young, to have it crash over me like the swell of a wave, finally coming up for air, after minutes underwater hunting for coins left behind in golden sand.

11. While Mahmoud Darwish's work has never been read more, or been more relevant than today, this stanza of his poetry has lived in a corner of my brain rent-free for years: "I am from there. I am from here. I am not there and I am not here. I have two names, which meet and part, and I have two languages. I forget which of them I dream in."

This liminal state, this in-betweenness, is a reflection of being human, where belonging is often elusive and identity is a patchwork of experiences. The two names and languages, symbolizing the constant negotiation between cultural identities, a struggle to reconcile the past with the present.

A testament to a place where the soul finds its anchor even when the body is adrift.

12. Mumbai, originally an archipelago of seven islands, started altering its bond with the sea soon after these islands were joined by reclaimed lands. The earliest records of reclamation are from before 1700 till 1918. This was also the period when Mumbai's crown jewel, Marine Drive, came into existence. The glimmering lights dotting the seafront that make up the majority of the city's postcards, also known as the Queen's Necklace.

13. A few Sundays ago, I sat on a bench in my neighbourhood, with my book, absorbing a rare, perfect day in the city. In this shared space bathed in sunlight, an Adidas clad toddler wiped his muddy palms on my bare knees, cracked a crooked grin and said hello. The motherless part of me

winced. The present version of me stroked down his sweaty curls and said hello back, in that voice you reserve for soft things—children, baby animals, someone stumbling over your language. With edges smoothed like sea glass, all rounded corners and gentle curves, a sudden burst of sweetness coaxed out of me, that wasn't buried as deep as expected, just when I felt I might be too salty to bear.

14. We often feel a strong urge to return home to rediscover our identity. As Alain de Botton suggests, architecture anchors our sense of self.

The ancient Greeks understood the profound connection between architecture and identity. Their meticulous construction of the Temple of Athena on the Acropolis, dedicated to grace and balance exemplifies this.

Without physical spaces, we struggle to remember who we are.

15. Wiping a spoon on my shorts. Flicking the kettle on. Hanging a damp peach towel on a clothesline. A puzzle assembled over days on the dining table, while waiting for the oven timer. Water dripping from a yellow watering can. Plates and bowls leaning against each other on the drying rack. Images of home as a pattern of normal things by normal people. The process of making and building a home is regular, from cavemen to society 6. Catastrophe averted with laundry detergent, with vacuum cleaners, a new vase, an IKEA Family Card (free delivery and assembly included). But when disaster knocks on the door, how do you answer?

16. Mumbai's relationship with the sea is a marriage. Tumultuous, beautiful and bitter, hostile and intimate. For better and for worse, in sickness and in health. A marriage of convenience laced with desperation. The sea is both a highway for trade, carrying dreams and cargo on countless dhows, and a relentless adversary. Rapid industrialisation and construction has impacted the city's relationship with its sea. Locals claim that the change in tidal patterns due to reclamation has eroded expanses of beaches, slicing it to narrow slivers of sand, far from the tidal pull of memory.

17. In Santorini, where the Aegean Sea unfurls like a cerulean tapestry, a pirate ship glides across the horizon, sails billowing in the dreamlike heat haze.

The scene evokes a nostalgic homecoming, reminiscent of Homer's *Odyssey*, or Wendy returning home from Neverland, a mirage cast by the sun-drenched, volcanic landscape.

18. Camus, when writing about the sea, often refers to Algeria with its seaside, as if it was a sensual being: it makes "kissing-noises." Being by the sea, life makes sense to Camus. "This is what the Mediterranean is—a certain smell or scent that we do not need to express: we all feel it through our skin."

When I travel to the Mediterranean, I carry two thin Turkish towels in my bag. One peach, one lemon yellow, so whenever the mood strikes us, we can lie down on the beach and let ourselves be carried away by spirits older and wiser than us, our roots both grounding us and letting us be transported by a breeze.

19. I visit one of my best friends and fellow *Mumbaikar* in Newcastle, where she has lived for years. She suggests a day by the seaside. We pull on boots and overcoats. We win candy called "Toxic Waste" at the arcade. We stare out at the sea, which is a pale imitation of what we used to know.

We indulge in *Lindisfarne* oysters, drenched in red wine and shallot vinegar. As we slurp it down, we close our eyes, tasting the ocean and its brine, feeling the closest we've felt to home, letting it linger on our tongue as long as possible.

20. Mumbai floods every year now, and the heaviest brunt of the disaster is borne by its poorest residents. According to NASA's Sea Level Projection Tool, as global mean sea levels increase each decade, Mumbai will experience a sea level rise of nearly 2 feet by 2100. In the mistaken belief that nature—especially the ocean—can be controlled and tamed, the city's relationship between its built environment and its ecologies need to be examined. Drainage systems that work are just the beginning.

21. I dream that I can speak in a third language. Of late, Italian has been the frontrunner. I spent the summer consuming the words of Elena Ferrante, Natalia Ginzburg and Jhumpa Lahiri; or rather the translations, wishing I could read them in the original, transported to an Italian summer 3 years ago where I jumped off a cliff in Cinque Terre, into the ocean.

Fear erupted on my skin, goosebumps on my arms and legs, toes flexed taut. The ocean has no bottom to imagine, no rectangular tiles to map, no lanes to follow, only vast depths and an uncertain horizon from where light glimmered. I weaved in between fishing boats, singleminded in focus, to find the face of someone I love, waiting on the shore.

22. I roll words with my tongue, softly and with care, like a tiptoe: *Dov'è mi trovo,* that's where I am. *Di dov'è sei,* where are you from.

23. My husband asked me to marry him by the ocean. He planned it that way, for reasons I never really needed to question. The ring was a silver olive branch designed by Paloma Picasso for Tiffany. He liked it because it was affordable, and came in the signature Tiffany blue box which I still keep on my nightstand. I love it because if you squint, it looks like a wave.

24. Of late, the romantic reality of the city's residents enjoying the beauty of the sea, by walking on the promenades or sprawled on the sands with chai is a sight less frequent. Barricades have been erected for constructions of freeways and coastal roads promising to "connect people and places." It smells more like stone and cement, than the sea salt and roasted corn sprinkled with chili and lemon that I remember.

25. It wasn't an ache I felt, submitting the paperwork to change my citizenship, it was a dart. A bite, with fangs. A sea creature seeking vengeance, Ursula with a stolen trident. Sharp pain painted in every shade of blue; like Chowpatty at sunrise, like Carter Road at sunset, like Bandstand at midnight.

26. Out of water emerges a city, Atlantis rising from the waves, that residents and lovers still call Bombay.

27. Bombay blue is my favourite color. The color of my toenails every summer. The color of tarps covering the city in the rain, the subject of "BLUED" by artist Sameer Kulavoor, gifted as a wedding present by an old friend the city gave me as a gift, many years ago.

 The color of afternoon twinkling into evening in London, the third time I'd met the boy who would become my husband and he said, "Oh, I'm from Bombay too."

 I re-read Maggie Nelson's *Bluets* that same week: "The half-circle of blinding turquoise ocean is this love's primal scene. That this blue exists makes my life a remarkable one, just to have seen it. To have seen such beautiful things. To find oneself placed in their midst. Choiceless."

28. There are seven seas and oceans or *Sapta Sagara* in Hindu mythology:

Lavanada (the salt ocean), *Ikshura* (the ocean with juice of sugarcane), *Surada* (the wine ocean), *Ghreetada*, (the ghee ocean), *Kshirada* (the milk ocean), *Dadhyoda* (the ocean of curd), *Svadudaka* (the ocean of sweet water).

29. To love what cannot love back is insanity. An exercise in heartbreak, a test of endurance. I have done it for years. I love, even now. A place of terrible danger and beautiful magic, it is tangled up in strands of my DNA, in the warmth of my skin, in feet that automatically move towards shores, wherever I am in the world. In Bombay, I loved and I became.

30. My last supper would be *Koliwada* prawns, a staple of the city's coastal cuisine. From Jai Hind, Highway Gomantak, or Pal's, these succulent prawns, accompanied by paper-thin chapatis and plain yellow *dal*, have been my inaugural taste of Bombay, regardless of arrival time.

    A ritual, a cornerstone of my visits to the city. The taste of the sea, infused with the city's distinctive spices, transports me through the decades, from childhood to adulthood. This culinary tradition, so deeply ingrained in my identity, has even crossed geographical boundaries, finding a place in my kitchen cupboards abroad.

31. Plato, the philosopher of light, depicted the oceans as a place of clouded understanding, of the base world of the senses. Plato's underworld, Scholtz writes, was "above all wet." It was a perspective that picked up on the deeply anchored image of the sea as a source of terror.

32. While I know definitively and without any doubt that Calvino's *Invisible Cities* is about Venice and not about Bombay, I can't help but also know definitively and without any doubt that it could be. A city like no other, a city made only of exceptions, exclusions, incongruities and contradictions.

33. Above our bed is a sketch of Marine Drive, little circles depicting the twinkling lights. It is in black and white, pen and ink. We imagine the blue.

34. Our suitcase groans. Inside, Santorini sleeps, not in souvenirs, but in stones, collected from Kamari Beach, smooth and cool. Fragments, curated memories, held in touch. The weight on the station floor lightens,

becoming a bridge to a languid, sunburnt afternoon, painted in dull gold washes. Anchoring the ephemeral, talismans of where I was, who I am and who I might become.

The pebbles live in two blue and white china bowls on our side table, collected from all the beaches we've ever been to. When friends visit, they're drawn to the bowls like moths to a flame, picking up a stone, turning it between their fingers, and tracing worn paths; when even the smallest pebble can hold the weight of a universe.

Is home the place you belong, or the place that belongs to you? Whichever it is, whenever I feel unmoored, a ship without an anchor, completely lost at sea, when I hold one of the stones close to my ear, I can hear waves crashing—and I'm home.

When a Man Tricked a Brook

CAROLYN JONES

1. HEADWATERS
Pedestrians stare curiously as I get on all-fours and peer into a storm grate.

"Can't see a thing," I declare.

My children mill nervously at my ankles, both on the lookout for schoolmates likely to smirk at a mother crouching on the street. Princeton is not a crouching-on-the-street kind of place. Nor is it a place for colorful homes, street food, dogs wearing neckerchiefs, unhoused people, or messy hedges. To be crumpled on the pavement like this—here, on a quaint backstreet of an affluent New Jersey college town—is a wildly irregular thing to do. But I can't help myself.

"Use your phone," my teen side-mouths. She's standing with her back to me like a bouncer.

Good idea. I activate the flashlight and dip my face into the grate.

"I hear dripping." My fourth grader joins me on the pavement and nudges my shoulders out of the way. In his mind, the sooner his mother solves her quest, the sooner he'll get what he came for.

What my son came for is chocolate fudge. What I came for is quixotic at best. I want to find the exact source of Harry's Brook, a medium-sized creek that starts in the heart of Princeton, flows through residential yards, meanders across the town boundary, and tips into Carnegie Lake. Almost a century ago, officials buried the first mile or so underground. I'm shocked by this, but a brief review of the history books suggests this wasn't odd. Everyone buried rivers back then; it was how you demonstrated progress.

Even in my homeland of Zimbabwe, a buried river flowed beneath my school. Still, I want to see exactly where it happened in Princeton.

The official who master-minded the brook's disappearance was the town engineer. His name was I. Russell Riker and newspaper clippings suggest he was proud of the interment. Harry's Brook had been flooding residents' basements for years. He had described the watercourse at various times as a ditch, an open sewer, and a health menace. This diversion of a dirty stream into a neat underground chamber gave Riker, a busy man, the relief of tucking a nuisance away.

As I drive with my kids into town to start our mission, I explain I'm curious to know how a man tricked a brook. That stream has flowed through the land for longer than settlers have been around, so by moral right, shouldn't it have resisted? After all, Harry's Brook shows up on maps going back to 1683. If the early stewards of the land, the Lenni Lenape, had kept written records, it would be in those, too. I tell my kids I like to imagine the natural world takes the long view on human decisions. Also, I want to see this engineering trick for myself.

Riker was shrewd. He took advantage of Works Projects Administration cash, a vast make-work program in the 1930s designed to pull Americans out of poverty. As he explained in a newspaper op-ed, public funds paid the wages of 68 local men, even during winter, when there would have been no other work.

Thus, during that penurious winter of 1936, grateful workers coaxed Harry's Brook into a concrete channel—a process called fluming—and slammed 860 horizontal feet of pavers on top. I may have over-imagined the engineering details but the effect is the same. The headwaters of Harry's Brook were buried underground, like a live body sealed inside a coffin. This section of the brook disappeared from the maps.

We park in the Spring Street garage, aptly named because the concrete structure for storing our cars was built near the source of our brook. I don't know what to tell the kids to look for because I suddenly realize I have no idea what to look for myself. We nose around the perimeter of the parking garage and peer suspiciously at the moldy walls of the bike shop next door. Then we venture onto Spring Street and eye the storm drains lining the street. I'm not sure what I expected from this outing—maybe a mini-waterfall tumbling into a cave? Riker said the chamber would accommodate a grown man, and I notice I'm seeking a gothic-type portal. I crouch on the road and holler into grates, my phone's flashlight slicing the dark. Once or twice, my children pull me from the path of an oncoming truck.

I do not find a portal. Nor do I find the source of Harry's Brook. But I do discover this: I don't know the difference between a regular storm drain and a buried stream. They both look the same to me. There are concrete walls beneath all those grates. Some have flowing water inside. But which of those channels belongs to suburban stormwater infrastructure, and which are the scene of a trick? Without a civil engineering degree, I cannot know.

I buy the children their promised fudge and wonder why I'm obsessed with this brook. It doesn't run through *my* yard, and to investigate its path requires me to poke around in other people's troubles. I'm not that kind of person. I'm a privacy freak and a coward to boot, so the thought of breaking norms or crossing property lines feels transgressive. As my children lick their chocolate-y fingers, I try to locate the source of my fixation on Harry's Brook. It may be this.

II. INFILTRATION

In 2018, two years after my partner and I bought a house in Princeton, our basement flooded. We had been woken by the thunder of a violent Memorial Day storm, but the drumming downpour that followed soothed us back to sleep. It was only after breakfast that I descended the basement steps to discover a pond. The storm had long moved on but here were our belongings floating in muck. Among the things lost were my childhood journals, as well as my wedding dress, which still bore my father's shoe-prints after our clumsily sweet father-daughter dance.

As I crouched in the slop in my rubber boots, I ran my finger over the purple-inked scrawls of my youth. They had turned into plummy smears, never again to remind me what it felt like to be a kid. I could not bear to touch the blackened wrack lines that had settled into the folds of my wedding gown. I'd thought I'd have that dress forever. I had not anticipated such loss.

I called my mother in Harare. She had kept her own wedding gown safe and I could still feel the swoosh of those 70s bell sleeves on my little-girl arms. She commiserated about the damage, but could offer no advice. Flooding had never happened to her. Not only do Zimbabweans not have basements, but too little water is their daily problem. A celebration for my parents is when a rainstorm fills their catchment tanks. They could only dream of a downpour like the one that had visited me. I turned to my neighbors instead. But despite two years of neighborly concord, none would look me in the eye. When I asked directly whether their basements had flooded, they deftly changed the subject. I realized I had bumped against a hidden boundary line, a cultural taboo I did not yet understand. I had to find my way by touch.

Soon after the waterproofing specialists dried our basement, they noticed the walls had been coated in a water repellant paint. Had the previous owners omitted certain facts? When I mentioned this to a realtor, only her eyebrows moved. It seemed the more I asked, the more unspeakable this underground water became. It was as if I were asking Princetonians to dish their filthy secrets.

Luckily, the specialist was happy to talk. He was a cheerful guy from North Jersey and as he folded our $7,800 check and tucked it into the pocket of his polo shirt, he explained the concept of hydrostatic pressure. Underground water seeps against your home's foundations, he explained, until the force breaks through your concrete boundaries and bursts into your home. He would seal our basement envelope, he promised. But the only way to truly protect our home was to stop water from arriving in the first place.

I considered how one neighbor's ivy slid over the boundary line to claim my viburnums, how another's neglected tree leaned toward my son's room, how gas-filled mowers fumed my Friday afternoons, and how someone's cat harvested my backyard birds. I noted that my fast-growing birch was shading my neighbors' tomatoes. Neighborliness was more complicated than this man implied. And worse, the residents of my street—warm and welcoming as they had been so far—would not acknowledge the water.

I read in the newspaper that the municipality wanted us to manage our stormwater runoff on site. But our plot was too small to hold it unless we turned the yard into a detention basin. Our basement specialist reassured me. With the steady optimism of a man making coin, he sunk several PVC pipes beneath our flower beds, dislodging the phlox that was just coming into bloom. The pipes slithered beneath the path we'd laid to draw guests toward our goldfinch yellow front door. Now there was a secret beneath their feet.

The next time it rained, the system worked just as my specialist had predicted. I heard the grinding of basement pumps, followed by guttural gurgles beneath the catmint. A churning noise preceded the splat of water being discharged beneath a holly onto the lip of the street. Like a guy popping up from a manhole to dump his trash, the cap on our outlet pipe snapped open to vomit water. From there, our runoff flowed downhill toward the street's storm drain, which chaperoned it quietly beneath Princeton's roads until it emptied into Carnegie Lake. During storms, I learned to listen for the pock of that popping lid then breathe, knowing the instabilities of the earth were whisking beneath my feet.

III. DAYLIGHTING
What exactly is a brook, I wonder now, as I pick my way through sliding mud. Is it just a moving puddle, or does it have properties known only to hydrologists? As I approach Harry's Brook, a plump squirrel eyes me warily from a branch. A chipmunk skids so quickly down a nearby trunk that it's surely done the animal equivalent of clutching its pearls. But I don't mind because it's lovely here. The water is babbling over the scattered rocks on the riverbed. Tulip leaves blade from the earth and a copse of snowdrops down on the banks remind me that, despite my frozen hands, spring is almost here. A tufted titmouse flutes from afar.

I move toward Harrison Street and another bird calls from an overhanging maple. My father, with his keen ears and leaf-piercing gaze, would know what it is. But I can't identify it because a convoy of dump trucks are now huffing down the road. It's suddenly less bucolic here. The brook water is murky and troubled by trash: plastic bags, squashed beer cans, a tire. Always a car tire. But I'm not worried because I'm now quietly elated. I've found the town engineer's portal, or at least, the back end of it. I'm staring at the mouth of the tunnel that brings Harry's Brook into the light. It's a wide concrete oval. A strange shape, I think, as if a giant stepped on a pipe. Nonetheless, Riker was right. A shortish man could stand up in it.

Gray water is rushing out of the pipe and cascading into the channel bed that becomes Harry's Brook. I marvel at this moment of transformation. It's no longer runoff in a sewer; it's streamflow. The moment feels significant, metaphorical, birth-like. While the water moved through the concrete chamber, it had been a town secret. But at this place on the edge of one of Princeton's busiest streets, it becomes known. Here is where

Harry's Brook starts, and if you believed the maps, you would think you had found the headwaters. But in fact, this is where the brook becomes itself. There's even an urban planning term for this act of removing manmade impediments from a river. Daylighting.

I reverse my steps along the banks so I'm moving with the flow of the water. An apartment complex abuts one side and all the units have PVC pipes poking from their foundations. Thanks to a recent downpour, the pipes are doing their part to fatten the brook. I follow the flow as it glistens into a stone archway beneath a road. When it emerges on the other side, it meanders through the properties of private homes. Up ahead, a wooden bridge bisects the brook, but I can't reach it without trespassing. Instead, I nose my way along the street and crane into strangers' backyards. On this fresh morning, I can see why Princetonians might have wanted a whispering brook at the edge of their property. Or at least I could, back when people believed themselves to be innocent.

I follow the brook until it disappears again beneath another road. Now it has vanished from sight and when I get home, I follow its progress online. Its path becomes a delicate blue vein coursing between the homes of the Littlebrook neighborhood, which had been built after Rikers buried the brook. On occasion, a house appears on top of where the brook should be. In others, the water glints back into the map images like a wink, just enough to show that it's still there and is now chomping at lawns and nibbling basement edges. I study the names of these roads. Snowden Lane, Rollingmead, Poe Road. When it rains heavily in Princeton, these are among the places that flood.

IV. FLOODPLAIN

Like the rest of the east coast, Princeton is gradually waking up to the idea of floods. Hurricane Floyd in 1999 shocked residents with how much water could gush through the town. In 2005, the municipality wrote its first flood management plan. Seven years later, Superstorm Sandy showed how quickly the creeks would rise. Property damage began to tick up from ordinary storms, now so much heavier than before. Soon, residents were seeing the connection between a warming world and all that rainfall sheeting off their roof.

But none of that had yet filtered down to me. At the start of my quest, I was still trying to solve the mystery of why my basement had flooded, especially since according to the mythology of my street, it had come for me alone. Except I started noticing green discharge caps on the edges of several yards. They were in other neighborhoods, too. We were a community of popping lids, it seemed.

Soon after, letters began to appear in the newspaper. "We have too much underground water," one writer said, adding that over-development made it worse. She referred to the prevalence of *teardowns*, a violent word to convey how people felt about post-war cottages being replaced by larger homes. Their increased footprints reduce the opportunities for infiltration, she explained, meaning the "the resulting excess will tend to flow into someone's basement."

I looked up from my newspaper. In my neighborhood, you would struggle to find a post-war house that hadn't expanded. But it was true that the new houses were bigger than the rest. I'd sensed community tension about them, as well as tentativeness, because the occupants were our neighbors, and many had become our friends. Could the nearby owners of one of those homes, the ones with the solar panels and the cute kids, be responsible for my drowned wedding dress?

An economist would call that unpriced side-effect an externality.

I'd call it awkward.

After a spring storm, a basement cafe not far from the Spring Street garage flooded. Soon after, it went out of business. Letters in the newspaper began to complain about Harry's Brook.

One nearby resident wrote: "In the last decade, what used to be called 100-year floods have, for some of my neighbors, become five-year, two-year, or even one-year floods."

On my street, a soggy mountain appeared on the asphalt outside a neighbor's home. The shiny trucks of basement waterproofers cruised town like crocodiles.

More letters appeared in the paper. "The town needs to act responsibly in addressing water problems," someone wrote.

Another neighborhood resident whispered that her flooded basement had created a sinkhole beside her foundations. I began to understand that this secrecy had something to do with money. Oh no. Had my big-mouthed questions about my basement unwittingly lowered the value of my home? Green outlet caps soon appeared on my neighbor's lawn. Next to my own pop-up lid, I planted inland sea oats, which I'd heard were thirsty.

My family and I went away on a long trip, and when we came home, I found a crop of cattails looming inside my hydrangeas. A passing neighbor asked if we'd built a pond. I imagined the ground softening beneath my feet. Those reeds love wet feet, he explained, causing my eyes to take on the shape of two eggs, which led him to delicately wonder if there was an underground spring beneath our yard. Underground springs in Princeton? I'd never heard of those.

It is a poorly-submerged fact that Princeton is built above a lattice of brooks. Five waterways flow through Princeton, and three, including Harry's Brook, claim their headwaters within the confines of our tidy little town. After the neighbor whispered about the underground springs, I zoomed into a street map and studied the path of these creeks. Harry's Brook wended through the Littlebrook neighborhood, but there were no creeks moving through mine. I turned to a floodplain map. Via pink shading, it indicated which properties were at risk of floods. The Littlebrook homes alongside Harry's Brook were a study in salmon, but again, none in mine. Oh, wait. I spied a smudge of pink two blocks north of me. I knew that place. It was an open ditch running between houses near my son's school, and it turns into a pond during storms. I laced up my walking shoes and went over to study this nameless ditch. It vanished into a culvert beneath Cedar Lane and never reappeared. Yet if it followed a straight course, it would run up against the foundations of a big new house, which sat squatly near the property line. I stared at the home's fashionable black window-frames, willing it to dish secrets about its basement. The house held tight to its underground news.

More letters appeared in the newspaper. At a public meeting the assistant town engineer, a sanguine man named Jim Purcell, told us that Princeton has a high water table. He said he had heard people describe Harry's Brook as the "flashiest creek in America." Then he admitted he didn't know where all Princeton's underground springs were. This destabilized me. What if I'd bought a house on top of one of these mystery springs? I had been seeking solid ground ever since I'd reluctantly left Zimbabwe after political chaos in 2000 had caused millions to cross borders in search of another home. Had I made a strategic mistake?

I began to feel an itch. The itch led me to a thirst for information that might explain why my new home was less solid than I had thought. It was during this time I learned about Harry's Brook's banishment underground, and the idea of knowable secrets hiding beneath my feet took on a psychological shade. I did not understand myself. In compulsive internet searches, I stumbled upon an obscure municipal document that stated a desire to daylight buried creeks. I wrote to Purcell, the sanguine engineer, to inquire where he would be conducting these daylighting operations. I had hoped to receive by return email an underground map, preferably with a hidden stream flowing toward my house. Perhaps sensing the frenzy of a crank, Purcell did not write back.

I became obsessive. I studied maps of wetlands, gradients, soil types. I examined the construction of Carnegie Lake, which framed the southern rim of my neighborhood. I looked at flood insurance rate maps, climate models, streamflow maps, federal disaster claims. I asked Purcell for a map of the storm drains in Princeton. He replied, via a proxy, that he did not have one.

So I digressed some more, branched off, tumbled into sinkholes. I combed through historical records to learn whether any forebears had mapped underground springs. I skimmed a stack of indigenous oral histories in case the Lenni Lenape had tales of the watercourses they fished and forded. An Early American historian suggested I examine property records. Colonist landowners had a financial incentive to mark every rock and stream, he advised, but I could not find detailed maps of the tract relevant to me. I did learn, however, that the first European settler, Henry Greenland, had mapped Harry's Brook because it passed through his land. Back then, it was called Henry Greenland's Brook. Historical records do not say why it changed its name to Harry. But by all accounts, Greenland had been a cruel and dishonest man. It struck a sour note that Princeton had given him the honor of naming this brook.

One evening in September 2021, the edge of Hurricane Ida passed through Princeton. I sat in my lightning-flashing kitchen and listened to my pumps kick into gear. I compared the volumes pounding my roof to the tropical storms I'd known in Zimbabwe as a child. But like all things in my American life, my personal archive held no precedent for this moment. Not far away, swollen creeks were flooding homes and trapping drivers in fast-moving waters. 91 people died. Included among them were people from towns near me. Among those drowned in rising floodwaters were Cheryl Talke, Hongzia Li, Malathu Karek, Suzie Hamra, Dhanush Reddy, Shyam Pula, Daphne Lopez Del Bono, Mark Pavol, Yvonne Mahoney, and Barry Snyder. Perhaps like me, they had not known such a terrible thing was possible. As they fought for their lives, my drainage system worked harder than it ever had. Yet despite all four pumps pistoning through the night, moisture bled through the seams of our foundations. My partner and I stood guard with thick brooms to sweep water into the sump pits. As we watched our basement puke into itself, and before I even knew how many of my fellow New Jerseyens had drowned, a cold panic seized my chest. These storms will only get worse.

V. DELTA

"This brook was alive when the Lenni Lenape lived here, right?"

My son and I are leaning into a biting wind as we stomp along a sidewalk running parallel to Route 27, a busy thoroughfare connecting Princeton to the neighboring hamlet of Kingston. The traffic is so loud that we shout to make ourselves heard.

I've coaxed my son into this unromantic scene because I don't want to find the mouth of Harry's Brook by myself. He and his sister have endured months of my slowing the car to peer into road-side creeks; of interrupting conversations to point out a storm drain; of venting my frustration at not being able to find the original name for Harry's Brook. It seems only fair that at least one child be with me as I close out my quest.

For close out I must. I have come to accept I will never know why my basement floods. In my drive to locate the source of the water, all I have found are tantalizing inlets, trunk lines, and outfalls—but no map, no system, no explanation. Unlike Harry's Brook, which has a clear beginning, middle, and end, my mysterious seep comes from everywhere at once.

My son and I edge along the sidewalk until we're standing at the spot where Harry's Brook flows out of the Littlebrook neighborhood, passes beneath Route 27, and flows into Carnegie Lake. Officially, this section is called a delta, but all we see is scrubby vegetation and scattered trash. American robins chitter at us from the branches of a river birch. Seagulls wheel above the lake. A storm is coming and flood warnings have already been issued. I imagine the drama of this location in a few hours once the lake has risen with the runoff from our elegant town.

We move off the sidewalk and down to the bank of the lake. A pair of Canada geese clack away as we allow the water to lick our toecaps. Our town engineer is working on a plan to create a stormwater utility. It will help Princeton manage all this extra water, as well as to pay for the infrastructure a livable future demands. At least Princeton's water puzzle is not mine alone, I think with relief.

My son pulls his jacket tighter around his chest while I admire my neighbors' pricy homes on the edge of the lake. Last year, the state of New Jersey passed a law requiring homeowners to disclose to buyers if their property has ever flooded. Perhaps this means we no longer need to fear that stormwater talk will tank our biggest investments. We're all sinking together. I wonder whether my partner and I would have still bought our home if we had known the basement would flood. I wondered why the sellers had not warned us. But then I suddenly know why. There had been no script for that conversation. I turn away from the water. We are good neighbors to one another in this town, I realize, but stormwater makes a mockery of our norms. Our runoff crosses boundary lines like a thief; it invades our private domains. Stormwater forces us polite Princetonians to acknowledge what we don't want to see.

My son finds a handful of stones and starts flinging them into the lake. What don't I want to see, I wonder, as I turn back to admire the vitality of his overarm throw. Princeton is his foundation, even if it does occasionally flood. The wind tousles his hair and he suggests we go home. Home. My journals—the record of my Zimbabwean childhood—were wiped clean in that Princeton home. My throat catches as insight seeps in. Gone too are my father's shoe-prints. At my wedding, we had danced to Neil Diamond's "Sweet Caroline" because it had been my parents' song for me. Whenever they played it, they would turn up the volume and beam at their little girl. I was their treasured child, one who grew up just in time for her country to explode and scatter Zimbabweans everywhere except home. I turn with my own treasured child as we head toward the car. Over my shoulder, I take one last look at the timeless brook that becomes a lake that becomes a river that will turn into the ocean that separates me from my first home. That's okay. This water flows on and on and on. Despite us, it always will.

A Tidal Triptych

R. D. SALMON

I
Sea View

A MAN NAMED JIM is kneeling in my kitchen. Jim is speaking in low, encouraging tones to the boiler, as he tries to coax it back to life. I can't make out exactly what he's saying but there is something about his calm demeanour that helps me to feel more relaxed. He is surely the *Boiler Whisperer* and all may yet be well. I hope so. I have felt cross all morning. This is probably because I have been cold all morning.

Since I moved into this house three days ago, the weather has turned. I sense the imminence of shorter, darker, sharply unforgiving days. I have so much to do but the cold, which crept into my bones overnight, has settled there, unresponsive to the multiple layers of clothes I've grabbed from the top of a yet-to-be-unpacked box and pulled onto my unwashed body. I can move only slowly, clumsily and because of that, feel even colder.

Jim shifts into a squatting position and looks up at me serenely. "I can fix this."

I wave my sausage arms in appreciation—Yay!

"But I need to collect a part. I reckon this boiler, given a little TLC, could see this house to the end of its natural life."

"Pardon me?" My sausages drop to my padded sides and rebound slightly from the cushioning.

Jim stands up. His tool belt jingles cheerily as he replaces some sort of wrench into its allotted loop.

"The village of Borth has been built on a strip of shingle; on one side you have the sea, on the other the marsh and joining the two, a tidal estuary. You are pretty well surrounded—waterlocked rather than landlocked." He releases the ear flaps of his furry hat and then, pulling on his gloves, chuckles. "It really is only a matter of time. Water always wins in the end, you know." Our eyes meet. "Don't worry," he hastens to add, "things should be good for another thirty years or so. Besides, you're just renting the place aren't you, so, er, no problemo! I'll be back in an hour!"

His long stride has already got him to the front door. He ducks to get outside, as he must have to do to get through most doorways. We see the world from very different perspectives. I follow him out and the cold nips at my face, relentless and distracting. I'm sure that I have questions for him but his van is already noisily belching and off he goes.

Thirty years. Are thirty years a long time? I consider how quickly my last ten years have vanished. Could thirty years be enough time to organise a village to move on with all pets, people and pianos intact? I have wanted, forever it seems, to live by the sea. I'm not over-committed if I just rent. I guess I'm just testing the waters.

I stomp around the corner of the house and through the side gate to access the scrubby, wind- and salt-scorched garden.

There, on a concrete base, is the oil tank. The tank is a shade of green which clashes with any conceivable shade of garden green. The ailing boiler runs on oil which is delivered twice a year. There is no mains gas to this area. This fact suddenly lends a greater sense of impermanence to the scene. If a village isn't worth a gas line—is that because people have long known that this couldn't last? Is the ground so unstable from the merging pressures of water shifting with the tides, nudging sand and soil, that gas pipes are out of the question?

I retrace my steps and enter by the front door, on a mission to dig out some gloves and a woolly hat before Jim returns. With some difficulty I shake my boots from my multi sock-layered feet and make my way up the wonky wooden stairs.

The entire house is on a slight slant because of subsidence over time, but it is on the stairs and landing that this becomes most evident. Here, the sensation is akin to being on board a slowly listing ship. The landing has a gradient all its own. As I come up here, I reach out a hand, automatically, to run along the old oak panelling, so like a ship, like an old, creaking ship, temporarily grounded but only temporarily so, if Jim's predictions hold water. I imagine the house giving up the ghost and betraying me to the sea. I was only ever a tenant after all, there can be no claim to permanence in that. My mind's eye conjures a picture of myself, like an extra in a disaster movie, tossed overboard but clinging for dear life to a length of this blessed panelling. In between choking gulps of salty water I'd surely be cursing my romantic ideals of coastal living. *A village built on a strip of shingle!* Whatever were our forebears thinking?

I pad into the master bedroom. This room at the front of the house commands an astonishing sea view. I pick my way through the muddle of boxes and bags to reach the elegant window seat. Upon this, already arranged, are cushions, a blanket and my binoculars. Instantly I feel better.

This view, through this window, was what first pulled me irresistibly into the house. Past the hopeless garden, the antiquated services, the wonky stairs and listing landing, I have made my way to this window seat and here have whiled away unproductive hours, transfixed by the tableau before me that changes, second by second. The tides of the sea, of the cold Irish sea, a rumpled sheet of teal silk, rippling, surging, advancing, regressing, tireless, timeless, bird and foam bespeckled. This morning there's a gaggle of hardcore, all-season surfers visible against the mustard smudge of the shoreline, slick as seals in their wetsuits.

A loud 'rattety tat tat' sounds on the front door. Pulling my gaze downwards towards the road I see Jim's van. How has he pulled up without my noticing? Can an hour have passed so soon? I'll go and let him in and then start my search for hat and gloves. I am dead cold now. While I was sea-gazing, my body took the unilateral decision to divert all blood away from my extremities.

I hobble back through the undisturbed chaos of the room and head for the landing, my arm reaching, hand outstretched to steady myself as I try in vain to hurry along on alien feet, my cold-numbed fingers bumping dully against the aged oak. The stairs creak beneath. They can tell me nothing of the lost sixty minutes but still, I know what I know about time and tide.

II
Low Tide

What's the strangest thing you've ever found on a beach?

Today, I found a naked Ken doll wedged in a prehistoric tree stump.

This Ken looks a little worse for wear. Evidently last night was a rough night. Like a groom after a stag party, dazed, naked and far from home, even his plastic hair looks dishevelled. I extract him from the sucky sand in the central well of the stump, give him a little shake and stuff him in my pocket. I imagine him warming up in there and feeling relieved, his tiny, chiselled features peeking out, safe now to gaze soulfully at the distant sea; the distant sea that has carried away whatever secrets it holds of his fall from grace.

Four or five thousand years ago, this part of Wales was not coastal, but an expanse of forest. As ice melt poured into the oceans—an enthusiastic host overestimating the capacity of the punch bowl—land was subsumed by sea and the forest was no more. Well, almost no more. From time to time, turbulent weather causes shifting of the sand, and the remains of the peat-preserved tree parts are exposed to light and air. They are not fossilised, and they will not last indefinitely.

There is something other-worldly about the sight of the forest when it emerges for an encore. Visitors stand mesmerised. If they were previously unaware of the forest's existence, there is an interval of cognitive dissonance to be processed before the 'wows' and 'ahs' are exclaimed. Awestruck is not too strong a word for this moment of realisation. This prehistoric forest is awesome. Natural phenomena command this word that is so misused in countless day to day exchanges. Perhaps we long to be awestruck and try to conjure the feeling with the incantation of awesomeness during our day-to-day mundanity. I think Ken might disagree with me. Isn't everything supposed to be awesome in Barbie world? But not last night—ha!—he is surely too grateful to complain.

These days, people look, exclaim, and then brandish their phones in order to Instagram and Facebook the hell out of this novel experience. Such collective outsourcing of memory assimilation may gain us something in terms of quantity, but what intangibles might be lost in the process? As a permanent resident now, I can restrain myself from reaching automatically for my phone when the beach is putting on a floor show. Consequently, I can feel a little smug and superior but still, back at the wonky house, I drink in the sea view with an urgency and avidity which confirms my addiction and should keep me humble.

There have been occasions when researchers exploring the site have found footprints of people dating from the Bronze Age. Who hasn't tried out other people's footprints for size on a beach? It is a common quirk of beach walkers—there is something irresistible and connecting and, one way or another we are surely all just visitors, sightseers, passing through.

"If you are squeamish," wrote Sappho over two thousand years ago, "don't prod the beach rubble." She must have known what it was to take a nice stroll, toes sinking into the sand. Hers are the words of an experienced shore stroller, and her advice is sound, but sometimes curiosity gets the better of any beachcomber. This is especially the case when low tide follows a good storm.

Just a few hours ago, the sea was here, right here where I'm walking. Any and everything that was swimming or sloshing around in it ran the risk of getting left behind. The tide going out is the big reveal for sea-borne paraphernalia—a sand-based yard sale where the interested walker can peer and prod to their heart's content.

Now, a dark band of pungent debris scribes the reach of the earlier tide. Rope, netting, plastic containers, all interwoven in a jumbled mess—with lengths of seaweed, some of it short, bunched and bulbous; some of it long and wavy edged, lying still now. As the heat of a promising day draws away its moisture, this seaweed develops the texture of overcooked spaghetti, adhering to adjacent strands and surfaces.

Sometimes, air that has been advert-fresh is suddenly threaded with notes of decay, sickly and noxious. A nose can serve as an effective early warning system for something that is better left unseen. If I notice a cloud of flies pixelating the air, that is a good indicator of something that is by no means 'awesome.' Whatever is quietly decomposing nearby, I'll quicken my pace to get upwind of it.

Approaching the shore's edge where the sand is damp and rippled, I see many small jellyfish dotted randomly around, like spots shaken from a giant paintbrush. The rise in sea temperatures is resulting in more jellyfish, of different varieties, washing up on British shores. The collective noun for jellyfish is, delightfully, a 'bloom.' In water one can see the aptness of this word—flowerlike, graceful, translucent, fleshy petals and tendrils glide through their element. They are 98% water. Once abandoned by the receding tide to their air bound fate, they eventually evaporate. That feels like such an absolute end to something which lived and moved and occupied its place in the world.

People don't move around in beautiful blooms or graceful shoals only to quietly evaporate and leave barely a smudge behind. In groups we are crowds, gangs, throngs, factions, families.

Nature pays no heed to sentimentality, but my sentimentality persists, nonetheless. It accompanies me on my beachcombing expeditions; it is what made me need to rescue Ken from the tree stump and what has me shedding a salty tear when my mind wanders over a landscape of helpless and hopeless creatures.

I can't help but picture myself once more, clinging to that length of oak—the same wood from which countless human coffins have been fashioned—knowing that in the rising sea, I would be out of my element and losing hope by the second.

I remember, and am discomfited by the thought, that I am around 60% water, as was the Bronze Age person whose footprint caused such excitement.

My footprints, where the sand is water-logged, are fading fast in my wake and may well have disappeared entirely by the time I get Ken back to my place.

III
High Tide

Attraction, excitement, crescendo, surge and crash. The literal translation of the Mandarin word for *orgasm* is 'high tide.' I appreciate the directness of the Chinese in this matter. We need not look far to find sensuality in imagery relating to the sea. Imagine a spring tide—the highest tide—when the moon is at perigee, the closest point in its orbit around the Earth. Here we witness the effect of the moon as he passes boldly near, and the Earth's watery soul responds to his celestial overture with swell and surge.

As the moon tugs at the sea, so in its turn does the sea seem to tug at us, pulling us irresistibly nearer. There is an instinctual drift of walkers on the beach, down towards the water's edge or, when the tide is high, they pause in their progress along the sea wall and just gaze and gaze and are for a while, mesmerised.

Perhaps this has something to do with the quantity of water we carry in ourselves, responding to an elemental or gravitational pull. Maybe it is the attraction of the negatively charged ions that are produced by the pounding of the waves, and which make people feel that bracing, energising sense of seaside well-being.

Borth itself seems to be ailing, morphing slowly into a perpetual Sunday afternoon. So many family homes are now holiday homes, bought by people who can afford not to put all their eggs in one basket. The little village school, where children are taught through the medium of Welsh, is being threatened with closure.

Ken has hung around, forsaking Barbie and any other beach dollies for me and the creature comforts of the wonky house. I have fashioned him a toga out of an old cotton handkerchief and secured this with a small safety pin onto which is glued some green sea glass. Last night I had fish and chips and today Ken holds aloft a three pronged wooden fork. 'Neptune Ken' stands proudly in my window, staring, steadfast and unblinking, out at the rolling sea. I considered dressing him up as 'Canute Ken' but an eleventh century style outfit felt a bit ambitious. That might be a project for the winter evenings.

In wintertime, I hear the old boiler creaking and gurgling into life, burning the oil, the ancient fossil fuel that has been delivered by a dirty great lorry. As I sit here, I feel warm and cosy—a little guilty, but cosy. I have made a start on Ken's kingly breeches and have plans for a shirt and tunic to follow. The needle work is fine but the bright electric lamp I sew by extends my day artificially and is convenient.

The background noise of the sea washing and skittering over the shingle is rhythmic and lulling. This sound could persuade me that all is well and timeless and unchanging. But the high tides, they are getting higher and, climatic or climactic, the power lies, as ever, in the 'c'.

Water, Land, People - The Price of Progress

MONISHA RAMAN

Water

I CAREFULLY TREAD THE NARROW PATH cleared amidst the wild bushes leading to the Thalambur Lake in the suburbs of Chennai, a coastal city. My feet struggle for balance in the softness of the laterite, damp from the recent spell. The gate leading to the lake is locked and Narashiman, my companion for the day, shows this alternate path after seeking the required permissions. Like a precious jewel guarded in the recesses of the wardrobe, this water body is protected with fences and gates, carefully watched by the local people.

~

The strong scent of dung engulfs the air here and periodic moisture-laden wind interrupts this scent at intervals. I am reminded of my visits to Grandpa's farm as a child and the times I held my breath at the cow enclosure.

~

The lake, tranquil in its stillness, lays calm as the wind draws ripples on its surface, constantly flowing as if seeking something beyond its barriers. The surface of the water disperses the sharp rays of the mid-morning sun reflecting on it all the way to the edges.

I try to listen more closely to the lake through the sharp sounds of the wind. I only hear the koel lost in a song in the wilderness of the bank. As if on cue, an egret takes flight from a casuarina trunk partly submerged in the middle of the lake. A Tamil Lacewing hops around the tiny white petals of the Thumba flower (*Leucas aspera*) in mesmerising movements.

~

The quinquagenarian Narashiman talks about his youth when the lake's surface area was more expansive, the floodwater basins spread across the village and the times one stumbled upon a pond every few metres. He fondly recollects the interminable sound of darters, storks and pelicans, the migrant birds during winter months.

~

The suburban part of the coastal city is a vast network of lakes, ponds and other interlinked water systems. Much like the circulatory system of the human body, the water flows through the veins in the ground, empties into organs, and carries excess water to the power centre of the sea, which partly functions like the heart. Similar to a network of cells, these water bodies operate independently and as a collective. It is well known that 80% of the city was wetlands in the 1980s.

~

I have only known water that flows from the mountain tops—loud, effervescent, vivacious, like a bunch of toddlers at play. This stillness, the composed and tranquil persona of water, is alien to my senses, yet mystifying and inviting.

~

I am an encroacher on this land, this city, moving like a molecule across membranes with no definite purpose or function and this locality rich with water has been my home for three years.

Land

Before the turn of the century, Thalambur was a vast agricultural hub with an equal number of humans and cattle. Bordered by giant palm trees, fields filled with rice saplings, lentils and peanuts were a common sight. With its proximity to the shore, groundwater was always in abundance.

~

Thalambur is a vital village in the circulatory network of water and is named after *Thalam poo*, the screw pine flower that once was in abundance here. Its alluring fragrance is said to have attracted women and snakes, particularly cobras, and it was harvested for use in perfumes and red *kumkum*. Thalambur no longer carries these flowers or the lushness of the bygone era.

The neighbouring villages along the banks of other lakes have proof of their history in legends, inscriptions on ancient temple walls or folklore associated with these temples. If Thalambur has a history, it probably lies underwater.

~

The largesse of land and water was reflected in the smiles and hospitality of the people. The land gave in abundance here.

~

In *Ettuthokai*, a compilation of Sangam-era poetry, the ancient Tamil lyrical text (widely believed to be before 300 CE), the landscape is divided into five categories based on its geographical location. This device is called *thinai* and each of the landscapes depicted has a specific poetic attribute. The Thinai also describes the way of life in each landscape. The Marutham *thinai* paints visuals of bountiful pastoral lands, with ample ponds where water buffaloes lived in harmony with farmers and people were intertwined with the land like the double helix of the DNA.

People

The village of Thalambur and the surrounding rural areas were filled with landlords and agricultural labourers until the turn of the century. The villagers cultivated most of the year other than peak summer months and celebrated their local goddesses once a year.

~

The people prayed to the land before sowing and after harvest, anticipated the rain, held special poojas in the temples when they perceived sparse monsoon, made offerings to the sun God annually and had deep reverence for the wind that brought moisture and rainfall.

~

The lake, their life source, was secured and sheltered like a newborn. Women in the village bathed in its water, their saree petticoats tied above their chests, with herbal powders for soap. They chatted and revelled in the music of each other's laughter and songs.

~

The women worked in fields and in their homes, adorned their hair with *Thalam poo* and looked forward to the annual temple festivals when they dressed in brand-new silk sarees and jewellery. Their marriages were arranged when they were in their early adulthood.

~

People could read the minute signs—a change in the direction of the sea breeze, mist in the wrong month, an unusual amount of dew in the mornings and predict the weather changes accordingly. After several generations of close association with the land, one understands a terrain like a spouse of many decades.

~

Children were taught to face east, pray to the rising sun every morning, gently feel the ground with their fingers and whisper gratitude to the land.

~

After a few months of moving to this locality, I dreamt of a woman outside a thatched roof hut on a paddy field one night. She sat comfortably on a *charpai*, an Indian string cot with a hand fan on a sultry day. Strong gusts of wind disturbed the curls on her forehead, carrying away bits of kumkum forming a perfect circle on her glabella.

~

I come from a long line of farmers. I know the sentiments land evokes.

~

Sangam Poetry:

O farmer who has many buffaloes
And many grain silos as tall as
Mountains!

When you go with others to plant
Paddy grass in the water-filled field,
Please protect the sedge grass and
Water lily plants. The young woman
In our house, her hair thick and
Dark, will wear sedge grass as
Pretty bangles and the water lilies
As a garment.

- Ettuthokai, (Sangam era compilation) Natrinai 60, Thoongaloriyar, MaruthamThinai—*What the heroine's friend said as the hero listened nearby.* Translated by Vaidehi Herbert.

WATER, LAND, PEOPLE

Water

Narasimhan is lost in thoughts as I try to scan the edges of the lake holding water that sustains the entire village in the vicinity. Shaped like a malformed rectangle, parts of the boundary stretch beyond my vision. A few metres away from the edge of this waterbody, connected by land, lies the Karnai Lake. Gazing at the water, he laments that the lake has shrunk considerably and much of its sand was mined illegally in the last decade.

~

In the three years of my living here, the northern part of the lake was the first sight I saw every morning from my rented apartment constructed in its vicinity. The placid water, the ripples, the reflection of palm trees on the glass-like surface on a bright day, the turquoise that beams on a sunny day, the fossil grey that transmits cheer on a cloudy day are not new to my visual pathway. Yet, standing at the bank, this majestic water body appeases my mind in myriad ways.

~

This city has always had a problematic relationship with water. More often than not, it is in demand, sending a frenzy of tanker trucks exploiting the farthest corner of water sources like disorganised ants contesting for the last of cookie crumbles on the floor. At other times, after copious monsoons, water flows over the roads, streets and ground floors of houses and commercial buildings, submerging the foundations of progress.

~

Water has a perpetual memory. It remembers the patterns and paths of the ancient past.

~

Standing at the edge of the lake, I observe a drongo, now perched on the partly submerged branch of the casuarina with its head tilted up.

~

Water covers my ankles. I feel it for the first time.

~

I ask Narashiman if he has ever seen the lake bed. Yes, he says, a few years ago. That was unfortunate. He wonders about the longevity of the water body. The houses are multiplying like rats and we are all dependent on this source of water. The groundwater recharge system is in disarray, partly due to the buildings that have sprung up and partly due to the heedless extraction of water from the vicinity of the lake.

~

The pond heron, a patient observer who was camouflaged all the while, swoops past us spreading its white wings. At the far edge, a pair of white-necked water hens float in a blissful stupor.

~

I heard about the mountains in my mother's womb. The tales about peaks and streams were my bedtime stories. But until I moved here, I had never seen a water hen or a swamp hen. I am an encroacher on this land.

~

This life-sustaining lake has yet another face. Running parallel to its glory is the history of its dark side. It has held many a corpse in the last few years and witnessed the gory ends of several people, sending a frenzy of fear that rippled across the village.

~

Nobody ventures to the lake to revel in its tranquillity anymore and no women are bathing in its placid water.

Land - Water

On a drive around Thalambur or its neighbouring villages, one cannot miss several boards with Plots for Sale printed on them or hoardings announcing upcoming gated communities. Most of these properties belong to real estate conglomerates whose prime shareholders are politicians of the ruling and opposition dispensation.

~

In 1998, the Government of Tamil Nadu allotted 250 acres of land to SIPCOT (State Industries Promotion Corporation of Tamil Nadu) to develop an IT Park in Siruseri, an agricultural hub close to Thalambur. The council procured an additional 750 acres from the local farmers. Seven open wells were constructed to aid the running of this IT Park.

~

As with every developing township, administration and beneficiaries saw profits in the vastness that was untouched. High rises, swanky glass buildings, shopping malls and showrooms of high-end brands stamped this locality as an upper-middle-class territory.

To make room for this, several ponds, rainwater harvesting tanks and floodwater basins were sacrificed at the altar of development. Only those water bodies large enough to have names stayed. The powerless, insignificant ponds and waterholes with no names were wiped off, an aquatic genocide destroying the history of the weak.

~

Land ownership changed hands by the day. Some resilient farmers held on to theirs. The value of a patch of land skyrocketed and vast measures were caught in disputes. Some of the *poromboke* public land belonging to the village administration was discreetly registered as private and sold. Hitherto unused patches of public land were given a number, an identity and ownership.

~

Privatisation spread like a tumour.

~

Wells were dug in such lands with new ownership. Tanker trucks made a beeline to these wells. This water sustained most families and commercial buildings in what is referred to as the IT Corridor, the state government's solid source of revenue, the oesophagus of the city. If this corridor shrank, the city would be starved.

~

Water was denied its rightful place. Water became scarce. Then, the mad hunt for water began.

Land - Battle

Small patches of farmland resisted the new developments and continued to yield.

What remained of the past are the few banyan and beech trees scattered around lakes and roads, tall palms that lined the lake beds, teak trees often protected within enclosed spaces, the resilient neem that has the spirit of the city and found ways to survive no matter the odds and the odd casuarina on abandoned lands.

~

Prosopis juliflora found a way to spread its tentacles across the vacant patches of land. A water-intensive weed, it competes and wins with other species in any ecosystem. The rosary pea plant battles with it for space, climbing over neem trees, huts, and walls forming a rickety tent-like enclosure. Gulmohar and copper pod trees slowly seeped into this territory. Most locals do not know the Tamil names of the latter two trees.

~

The bright red and black beans of the rosary pea plant are often seen lying scattered on the sides of the road. It is used to treat wounds and scratches caused by dogs and mice. Before the advent of commercial buildings and the influx of outsiders, children used these seeds for their board games. Called *Pillaiyarkannu* in Tamil, two of these seeds are stuck as eyes on the clay idols of the elephant-faced God on the occasion of *Chathurti*, bringing life to the statue. God is shaped into existence and he sees most homes in the Tamil speaking land through these seeds.

~

I am an encroacher on this land. Yet, I know the sense of alienation that arises when the landscapes from memory, which defined the visuals of home, undergo rapid changes.

How can I tell my daughter the stories of this land, its beguiling intricacies and enigma, when I am largely ignorant of them? How can I try to understand the terrain that shape shifts ever so often?

~

Sangam Poetry:
Oh small white heron! Oh small
White heron with bright, white
Feathers like shore-washed clothes!
Come to our town.....

- Ettuthokai, Natrinai 70, Velliveethiyar, MaruthamThinai - *What the heroine said to a heron.* Translated by Vaidehi Herbert.

People - Land

The local farmers had mixed responses to this development. While some worried that the land that contained their sweat and that of their ancestors was wiped from their vision, others, especially the youngsters, rejoiced at breaking the intergenerational patterns of drudgery on the field.

~

The farmlands sought for housing societies and gated communities paid the farmers well. After several generations, the farmers who entered a new decade of the millennium were stripped of their identities.

~

The money brought along bigger, more comfortable houses and was deposited in banks and the interest supplied the income. The community that had lived on principles of minimalism for centuries could not easily flip over to extravaganza.

~

A few young men moved away from the locality to study and make a living elsewhere, while some sought employment in the city. A good number of them felt they did not have the need to supplement their family's income. They spent their days as a group, playing cricket in the open fields and spreading the word about land available for sale. Their income was meagre, but they were blessed with time for endless adventure without the toil and bustle of a peasant's life.

~

Meanwhile, there was a mass influx of white-collared labourers who spread across suburbia, much like the rosary pea plant, clinging and growing at the expense of native trees.

~

The people whose lives depended on water and land a generation ago were in flux. A few of them grew as leaders in the local administrative unit. Every leader groomed an entourage. Members of this unit controlled the sale of land in the vicinity and the construction of wells on the lands. Every development has to pass through them.

~

Unresolved disagreements have led to a few murders in the past, the bodies mostly dumped into the lake, their once sacred entity.

~

Sangam Poetry:
In the bright, vast backwaters
Where the killer sharks frequent,
Punnai tree flowers shower their
Fine golden pollen abundantly on
Gem-coloured, dark blue water lilies.
In the grove, where fragrant
Thazhai trees spread their flowery
Scents as the sun's rays fade away
In this evening hour, we
Are spared the pains of our disease
Which brings spreading agony.

- Natrinai 78, Keerankeeranar, NeythalThinai - *What the heroine's friend said to her.* Translated by Vaidehi Herbert.

Water, Land and People

In the first quarter of 2022, the Tamil Nadu Government made it mandatory for land registrants to give a statement that the plot presented is not a waterbody, a channel or catchment area. If the declaration is found to be false, legal action will be initiated. This ruling was timed two decades late.

~

Walls and fences were built around the Thalambur Lake. A rigid boundary was marked for water. The lake was ordered to be content with the few metres of extra land allotted.

~

Caught between a tranquil past and a directionless future, Thalambur and many of its neighbouring villages are clothed in chaos. More boundaries arose between the natives and immigrants, the wealthy and labourers, religious majority and minority, the employers and employed. Entertainment centres, shops and outdoor spaces were earmarked with these boundaries.

~

No human boundaries could contain the cattle.

~

Women slowly lost their privilege to revel in the natural bounty of this place.

~

Somewhere lost in this discord is a farmer who pays close attention to the direction of the breeze and watches the pattern of ripples on the surface of the lake, a woman labourer who dreams of a short slumber in the alluring shade of palm trees on the shore.

~

In the backdrop of *Marutham Thinai*, representing the pastures and fields, lovers and spouses quarrel endlessly. Despite a life blessed with abundance, mental conflict was writ large on this landscape, in this several millennia-old literature.

~

Perhaps land has memory.

From my window, I often spot a cattle egret looking skywards while babblers are always finding their symphony. For a short span of time, there is a sense of sublime and harmony in the air.

The Memory of Calmer Seas

CAITLIN CACCIATORE

"How often have I lain beneath rain on a strange roof, thinking of home."
—As I Lay Dying, William Faulkner

I. the sky was the kind of blue | that only ever occurs in dreams | and in movies | and in memory.

EACH SUMMER, I AM GRIPPED BY AN ABYSSAL TERROR that this year shall be the last year of life as we know it on this peninsula. The feeling comes earlier every year, arriving along with the onset of North Atlantic hurricane season and lingering like a bad omen all summer long and into the autumn months.

My hometown was the suburban Queens neighborhood of Howard Beach. On the night of Hurricane Sandy, the water stopped at my neighbor's door. My mother called it my neighbor's miracle. She told her as much, affirming that Angela "was a much better person" than my mother could ever hope to be. I don't know if that much is true; all I can remember is the feeling of those words sinking like a stone to the bottom of my well. Miracles come but once in a lifetime. Who is to say that the waters will be so kind as to stop just inches from our doorstep—again?

THE MEMORY OF CALMER SEAS

I stood on the sidewalk as the floodwaters retreated, pacing the sidewalk that had just moments ago been subsumed by water—putrid water from an already polluted bay into which sewage empties. Fate had spared us, yet I saw a different destiny unfold in the days and weeks to come. One where the water didn't stop. Other doorsteps, now portals to worlds that had been ruined—family photos weeping ink, sodden books, flooded antiquities, broken heirlooms, gaping holes where windows had once been, and damaged wood beams encrusted with the leavings of saltwater and sewage.

Of the sea, it's been said she is a harsh mistress, one with the capacity to rise up and flood streets you used to know, rising waters rushing past places you will no longer recognize to ravage parts that will remain unknown to you, in their time of dying.

Sometimes, I stare out at the ocean, wondering when the fury of the Atlantic will once again rise upon us and show us the wrath of water as it becomes a weapon. The city spends millions of dollars every year fortifying the beach. They built a sea wall, and I watched the CAT machines slowly crawling up and down the beach, little offshore rigs dredging sand from several miles out as the vehicles redistributed the sand like the industrious machines they were. But from afar, they looked small. Insignificant against the weight of a water-world where the sea could breach its borders at any given time.

I watched the wall go up. Sometimes, I allow the fear to creep in—that destiny will not be so kind to me twice, that I'll still be here, on this peninsula, when the next major hurricane comes to New York City's doorstep.

To those who live in Manhattan, Brooklyn, the Bronx, Staten Island, and even other parts of Queens, our ways are antiquated. The pace of life in a beach town slows to a crawl in the off-season, and whenever I travel inland, I am swept up in the ocean of passersby all moving so much faster than I, hurrying to and from work and running from problems I am not privy to. It's almost like relearning to walk. Here, we amble. We meander. I've never seen anyone who calls Manhattan their home engaged in anything slower than a brisk power-walk.

Yet for all their scorn—we are the first line of defense against any coastal storm. If the sea wall fails to hold the water at bay, yes, we will bear the brunt of the damage—we'll suffer the greatest number of causalities, the highest amount of property and vehicular damages, and infrastructure failures, but who is to say the water will stop at our doorstep? Borders at a great enough distance are indistinguishable from fiction, and if we flood, you flood with us.

II. I sometimes wonder | if you ever | got out of that town | I left | the better part of me there

I am leaving this place. I am already mourning it, even as I walk up and down the shoreline, tracking seagulls, raccoons, dogs, and people on their comings and goings. It's a game I play with myself. I see how far I can track a particular creature—human or otherwise—until their tracks veer off into the tide or are washed away by the sea or fade into the oblivion of the hundreds of others who have passed that way.

I prefer the beach in the off-season. There's too much foot-traffic to play my game of choice in the summer, and the heat deters me as well as the early morning beachgoers hoping to find a spot before the crowds come in. We call them DFD's. It's Rockaway slang for "Down For the Day." They come, they go back to their small Manhattan apartments with salad bars on every corner, and they leave behind a prodigious amount of trash that later gets swept to sea to choke some poor, bedraggled sea creature who is starving for sustenance in a sea of plastic.

I wish they'd leave only their footprints, intractable amongst the comings and goings of the thousands of people who come from all over NYC to enjoy the Rockaway's beaches, dining and shopping. There are seasonal shops that open only during the months when tourism is booming, seasonal food stands that shutter their doors once autumn sets in, and all other sorts of amenities that the locals are usually priced out of. We even have a spa in our new hotel, aptly named Rockaway Hotel because it's the only of its kind on the peninsula.

I live in a gentrified area. The city is in the final stages of completing a middle school in my development, so poetically named 'Arverne by the Sea.'

Every year, they pour more money into this sinking ship. And every year, more locals are priced out of the housing market, at least in the better parts of town. There's very clearly a 'right' side of the tracks and it's just as evident as when one finds themselves on the 'wrong' side of the tracks.

When I go, I'll miss this place. I already miss the parts of it that have been swallowed by the sea—long rows of houses slowly rotting away, gaping holes in their roofs exposing the emptiness that the boarded-up windows don't want you to see: the remnants of someone else's life, the place another human being used to call home, but now it's nothing more than an empty shell of a house slowly sinking beneath sea level.

I miss the sign—"Marina. Coming Soon." The marina never did arrive, and the sign was all but faded beyond recognition by the time they got around to taking it down. I mourn for the one and only bookstore on the peninsula, the one that just got off the ground as COVID was starting to rage in other parts of the world. I look back on the stores that are no longer in business and wish I could go there one last time.

III. these streets | have changed me into someone I don't recognize | the mirror | mocks me

Sometimes, I wish I could bottle up the feeling of the sea breeze on my face, the smell of salt and brine. I wish I could set it out to sea and have it return to me, one day, when I am least expecting it and most in need of it.

I'll miss the rainbows after summer storms. I'll miss the placid pace of life in a beach town, the ambling walk of someone who has set out to wander seeming to put a spring in every step. I'll miss the dragonflies swarming as they first hatch, wet wings weighing them down as they perform their dizzying, electrifying dance through the sky, buffeted on all sides by sweet summer breezes.

I'll miss the Monarchs, which are fewer in number each and every year. There used to be hundreds of them. Now, they migrate fitfully, in small groups that struggle valiantly against the air currents. One day, we'll see them flying up and down the coast for the last time, and then there will be no more Monarchs. They'll come and they'll go, never to return, their passage over the threshold of extinction marked by newspaper articles written by budding journalists whose children won't remember what it's like for a butterfly to alight upon their hand.

The things I'll miss most are pedestrian, quotidian—precious little gems of moments, swept away with the tide as it rises and then recedes, leaving sand and stranded sea creatures scrambling for tidal pools. The things I will miss cannot be bottled, bought, bartered, or sold—but they can be taken away. These precious things, we'll watch them burn—or else we will bear witness as they are drowned in a sea of sorrow so vast it cannot be contained by mortal means.

IV. you called me a hurricane | some storm | always looking for some
more distant city | to deface

Hurricanes are not known for finding borders to be barriers to their destructive powers. Such terrestrial things as city limits, redlined districts, state lines, even the sign that separates one borough from another—are inconsequential at best, fictive at worst. *Leaving Brooklyn? Fuhgeddaboudit.* At least the sign is rooted, anchored, moored to the ground. A hurricane could still topple it with ease but at least it could put up a token fight, shaking and shivering in gale-force winds.

Borders are a different story altogether. We often see a map of the world as it is in our minds, divided into sections we call nation-states, which will often go to war at the slightest hint of the golden opportunity to own an extra sliver of that map. But those lines aren't real. They're just stories we've made up to separate our tribe from all the others. It's quite similar to the lie we tell ourselves when we divide ourselves between the political right and left. The water doesn't care whether you are socially progressive or conservative. Climate change doesn't care if you believe in it.

When the floods come, when the hurricane arrives in all its spectacular fury, when the debris is lifted by strong winds and unpredictable updrafts, it won't discriminate between right, left, moderate; it won't care that your neighborhood has a higher average income than mine: it'll ruin your possessions and leave your life in shambles, all your laundry out to dry on the lawn to see if it can be saved; because that is the nature of hurricanes. The borders of the country you so love—the dashes dividing your borough from mine—county lines you've crossed countless times—none can be seen from the lofty point of view of the hurricane, its towering presence of looming clouds and the threat of rain, followed by the promise of flooding.

V. then you must be a sudden squall | a fleeting flame | the memory of
snow | slowly receding beyond the horizon

I will always keep the memory of this place and its people close at hand. When I am gone, when I have fled this place for New England—when my ship comes in—I will always remember what it's like to walk barefoot across the sand in any season. I'll remember the hoarfrost on the boardwalk, fractal patterns making me slip in the early morning hours, the city shimmering like a jewel in the furthest distance, and further still—the line of the horizon, unbroken save for the cargo, freight, and passenger ships traveling out at sea at a great distance up and down the coast.

I'll remember the first snow I experienced when I moved here, and the blizzard of 2021. I'll cherish the memory of planting dunes as part of my university's community service requirement. I'll cradle this place in my heart, even after it's lost to me, even after it's lost to time, to tide, to the next hurricane.

And I'll use it as a reminder, not to make the same mistakes of the generations before me. When the Rockaways is underwater—as the warming rises past the accepted limits defined by the Paris Agreement, as the sea rises with it—I will mourn it deeply. Of our stewardship over this world, I can only say this: we failed. We failed ourselves, we failed our children, and we have doomed countless species to extinction. We will never know the extent of biodiversity this planet once held. We took our Eden and bespoiled it. We kept the fires of industry lit for so long that the skies poured forth acid rain and the world started to warm, creating a cascading greenhouse gas effect which scientists warn cannot be stopped.

We found our one precious planet in a state of equilibrium. We were so fearful of one another that we became the barbarians at the gates, ready with our pitchforks and our torches and our outright refusal to believe in anthropogenic climate change or act to remedy it, even in the face of overwhelming evidence collected by the world's finest minds which prove beyond a shadow of a doubt that human activities are causing accelerated warming on this world. We'll find ourselves lifting our heads from where they had been buried in the sand just long enough to watch as the last embers of the world as we knew it are slowly extinguished, and we will weep openly in the pouring rain, cradling the broken remnants of flooded cities in our palms and carrying the weight of oases turned to desert on our shoulders. And what a terrible burden that shall be.

FIRE

FIRE HARDENING

CLAIRE ROBERTSON-PREIS

THE TREES OF MY HOME EXHALE the breath of other people's vacations. Fresh oxygen touches the faces of families wearing their jeans tucked into new cowboy boots. Sun-starched air brushes past a couple putting a new national park sticker on their RV. A gin and rosemary cocktail of fresh chlorophyll teases a fly-fishing man in waders. Like these tourists, I have also come home to "take in the air." I seek a cure for my 21st-century case of overconsumption in the highly photosynthesized air of my home.

A few miles outside of Missoula, on the road to my home, signs at each bank of mailboxes warn, "You are entering a *Firewise Subdivision*." The houses snuggle against a Forest Service section to the northwest and state land to the northeast. Roman Creek crisscrosses the hills, rilling year-round. Seen on a compass rose, 180 degrees of mixed ponderosa pine public forest press against the northern property lines. Western larch bend over the fences reaching toward our home and douglas firs drape themselves over our gate.

In the velvety night of 2 a.m., the trees crowd together darkly like so many choristers on risers. I slink quietly into my childhood room, delayed by my late start from Portland. I notice the heat as I flip on the window air conditioner, a new addition, and drop into an uncomfortably dry sleep.

In the bright light of morning, new gravel deposits in the yard catch my eye, strange paths blooming in concentric rings 3 feet wide. These ripples

FIRE HARDENING

travel outwards from the skipped stone of the building. One encircles the porch, the other delineates the outskirts of the yard inside the fence. I step barefoot onto the grass for a closer look. As I rub the sleep from my eyes, I imagine our timber frame home sinking into a whirlpool of gravel on the forest floor, flames licking the edge.

Over breakfast, I read in a pamphlet that these gravel fire defense rings should be made of poured concrete and 5 feet wide. Five feet of concrete for each ring sounds like too much to my father. Instead, he has created two sets of three-foot rings, separated by an entire flammable yard. On paper this might be plausible, but to my eye this looks about as effective as witchcraft. I silently wonder if this is much more than a circle of salt guarding against some future summoned devilry.

I wander between my warlock father's protective circles, coffee cup in hand. New tree stumps in the yard remind me of my missing wisdom teeth. My father feels the absence of the two doug firs deeply, who were sacrificed as part of a different protection ritual from the flames. He informs me that the largest doug, the guardian of our horseshoe pits, was in fact only 90 years old at most. He says that, prior to the offering of our "dangerous trees" to the fire gods, he thought they had been here at least 150 years.

A 150-year-old doug fir standing in this particular stand of forest would be deeply implausible following logging and fire suppression. Northwestern Montana's forests exist on a faster fire cadence than my late-arriving family understood. Both the tribal elders and the Forest Service agree now on this point, a breakthrough of understanding on the government's part that comes many fire seasons too late. The Salish caretakers of this particular forest, which grows on the hills between the Ninemile and Missoula valleys, used to set fires on the way to their autumn camp every year, curating late fall burns in the valleys. These fires combined with lightning-set fires in high summer to renew the trees. Crown fires were rarer than they are now. Flames cleared small thickets of young firs and thick stands of ponderosa pine so the mature trees could sunbathe in our short dry summers.

A full understanding of what we stole through fire suppression evades me, though I see evidence everywhere when I walk out the gate for a morning walk. I turn left on the first forest service road and thread through young trees growing too close together. I am sure this was logged sometime in my parents' lives, as the thicket of little ponderosa are all roughly the same height. Ladder fuels reach up unencumbered and brush the lowest boughs of the packed firs. Whenever I reach a rare meadow by an abandoned road, I brush my hands through the high grass. I bend the stems of the still green European oatgrasses that are replacing the local fescue, a bad habit that means I am leaving a trace. As I crunch back into the shade across layers of brown pine needles on the floor, I realize that my knowing this place intimately does not mean I know the way it should be, but I still love it here.

Prior to fire exclusion by white settlers, a given ponderosa pine or doug fir stand of trees might burn low and slow every 12-20 years. My parents have lived in this particular house for 12 years (which happens to be the longest we have ever been at one address), so they are due for a blaze any time. Truthfully, we know the flames are late in coming. We look out the kitchen window at all this fuel outside our gate and guess that this section of land last burned more than one hundred years ago. Maybe around the 1910s, we speculate, around the time my great-grandparents stepped off the boat and sank their own tap roots into the soils further east in the state.

I should have lived through two to three fire cycles instead of 30 roaring wildfire seasons. I meditate on what remains of our fir and count its tree rings. I do not know enough to differentiate earlywood and latewood or to learn definitively if or when the flames last touched the base of this tree. I can note which rings are narrower and wider, reckoning wet years and drought years until I lose interest after about 60 rings. I think my favorite tree, my reading tree, may have been unnaturally selected by the extermination of fire.

I decide to improve the fire barrier while I am here. Back from my walk, I start to shovel gravel from the pile only to discover it is too hot for yard work. At first, I deny the heat because I love summer in the mountains. I live for my return to the deep blue of cloudless skies and the sizzling scent of pine needles. In dry heat, when I sweat through a shirt, it normally evaporates and cools me. With childhood summers spent bucking hay bales on the flat, I can handle hot and dry weather. But before I finish loading the wheelbarrow I call it quits, the mercury well past 90 already.

Montana's hottest hour in the summer is about 4 to 5 o'clock. After I give up on adding gravel to the path, the heat only increases. It is even too hot to play on the water. I know from experience I'll burn my butt if I take a black inner tube bouncing down the Clark Fork in this direct sun. I do not want to jostle in the summer crowds on a paddleboard at Holland Lake or Flathead Lake and I don't want to pick up swimmer's itch from Frenchtown Pond.

Temperatures this hot also mean no horseback rides, except in the earliest part of the day. Another change from a childhood steeped in the smell of horse, when the salt of our exertions mingled with the pines. I miss the joy of chewing on a clover stem and holding a lead rope in one hand so my chestnut mare can graze as the sun dries both our sweat. The heat breaks the summer routine of curry comb, brush, check legs, flyspray, check hooves, saddle pad, saddle, and bridle.

With nothing else to do, I read indoors and seethe. I realize it's still 89 at 8 p.m., even though the house sits at an altitude of nearly 4,000 feet. I am not acclimated as I go to bed. Everything awakens me; the heat, the sleep paralysis demon I thought I left in Portland, and the roar of the new window air conditioner. By 2 a.m., I am aggressively alert.

It is still too hot in my nest above the garage, so I tiptoe downstairs onto the asphalt driveway. Under the vaulted ceiling of stars suspended by trees. I feel small in a familiar way. Looking up in the clearing, I recall standing on tiptoes to peek over the edge of the countertop in my grandmother's kitchen. Instead of reaching for the cookie jar, I grasp at the universe.

Looking up pulls back the curtain on the passing of time. Both distant stars and nearby trees offer physical proof of the river of changes passing by. I relearn a truth I first heard when I was eight from my father, who taught me to stargaze back when we lived on the flat in an old farmhouse. I imagine the sky is unchanged since we looked through the lens of our shared telescope. I remember tent camping in our field in September after the third cutting of hay, looking up together at constellations and blurry planets.

My dreams of being an astronomer, a meteorologist, or a scientist at all lie abandoned in college music classes. In adulthood, I prefer the celestial eternity of stars and stories to the arboreal timeline. A star that will blink out in 10,000 years (to our perspective on Earth) feels everlasting next to a paper-dry 80-year-old lodgepole. Somewhere a star can wink out unnoticed, its light reaching Earth until long after it's gone, the firmament is more permanent than this forest. In contrast, the oldest nearby tree I know of is the 1,000-year-old larch named Gus, who stands in a grove about 70 miles away.

The Milky Way shines brightly and Cassiopeia traces a "W" above the horizon. Draco wraps his tail across the top of the night. I note a change on my own timescale in the metered flash of manmade satellites, an observable difference from my childhood. Through the trees to the north, I find the Big Bear and Little Bear. I shiver, even though I do not need my light sweater. My feet are toasty against the retained heat of the asphalt as I look up at the stars. I read that, unlike concrete or gravel, some types of asphalt catch fire at only 200 degrees of direct heat. I imagine a myth where the forgetful sun leaves behind heat through the night, irritating the moon-god.

The next morning I worry that little terrestrial bears will go hungry, unlike their celestial cousins. I see the tiny Oregon grapes shriveling early in the season. The huckleberries are failing so I do not harvest any. I cannot pick one for me and still leave one for the bears and one for the bushes. The bears will need to go further down into the valley to feast on the fruit trees. Even though I won't be here, I remember September mornings banging pots and pans to shoo them away because a habituated bear is a dead bear.

The rest of the family trickles in as the day passes for a family reunion. The temperature has been over 100 degrees for four days and over 90 degrees for seven days consecutively. This is highly unusual weather. The brilliant sunset taunts us, the visible wildfire smoke drifting past other states and provinces, but the AQI is not bad here yet. So far, the only fire starts in Montana are east of Helena. At dinner, some of us are distantly sad for a firefighter on that blaze, a pilot whose plane crashed in a reservoir scooping up water.

I go outside to teach my niece and nephew, C. and E., to play badminton. In the twilight hour we are enthusiastically terrible. I share that a professional can hit a badminton shuttlecock over 200 miles an hour. T-ball flunkie E. wants to hit the birdie that fast. At age ten, his interest lies in whacking, yelling, and spinning, rather than in making it over the net. He makes contact with the shuttlecock only once, hitting it into a nearby pine.

A more willing pupil, six-year old C. is delighted with the attention. She makes it over the net occasionally, when she remembers to keep her eye on the birdie. Her laughter shimmers—one of the dogs has stolen the shuttlecock. She wanders off distracted, then cries crocodile tears whenever an adult tries to play using her abandoned racquet. The dads play me and my cousin with glasses of whiskey in hand. Our best volley lasts for 5 exchanges.

At 2 a.m. my sleep paralysis demon awakens me again and I sit up screaming. I stare at the ceiling for a bit before I go outside to gaze at the stars, partially obscured this time by a high veil of smoke. I think about teaching badminton and music and how it matters more that a pupil loves the subject. I would rather they find a sense of joy than find perfection. The heat of asphalt on my bare feet distracts me.

The next day of the reunion marks day 8 over 90 degrees and day 5 over 100 degrees. My partner goes to the new vegan, gluten-free donut shop near the college that's a 30 minute drive one way. They need a brief escape from my badminton pupil C, who now wants piano lessons in the cool of the house. The two of them spend over an hour at the piano before donut duty calls.

Meanwhile, the reunion is in full swing, and my mother reminisces about the weather. "This isn't that weird," she says. "When I was growing up, we did have hundred-degree days. Always on a horse show day! Or at the county fair."

I confirm the numbers for her. She is not wrong, the longest number of days above 90 for this town is 12 days, a record set when she was growing up in the 1970's. She crows with pleasure because she accurately remembered the heatwave. Her memory of past weather lets her crawl out from underneath the pressing now-ness of global warming.

I notice a key omission from the record conversation, but I don't want to yank her back to our shared reality. Although the consecutive days record from the 1970's still stands, it does not include 100 degrees days. There are so many ways to create a record, to experience something that hasn't been experienced before. I imagine a nesting doll of recorded temperatures, a perverse matryoshka of record daytime highs nesting inside record nighttime highs nesting inside consecutive records.

I know something about matryoshki from my Russian studies days in college, when I read *War and Peace* and *Master and Margarita* in the shade of the now-absent doug fir. I enjoy looking for patterns everywhere, and my favorite nesting dolls produce imperfect copies. I find my first matryoshka in my casual reading today, which is John Vaillant's *Fire Weather*. I remember reading my first Vaillant book, *The Tiger*, under that same tree for a course about the Russian Far East. Sitting on the stump, I open the cover and find the next doll to crack open in the subject matter. The heat increases and I drip sweat onto the page as I read about the disruptive relationship of Euro-Americans with fire.

Fire Weather reflects on our Promethean connection to petroleum through the lens of the Fort McMurray wildfire. An unmistakable irony of reading *Fire Weather* next to government land full of mismanaged timber is that my family's house was bought with petroleum money. Not big petroleum money—that's for the eastern part of Montana and the Bakken shale—but my parents worked in the industry. My mother and father had to leave Montana after college, priced out by the dying economics of family farming and Butte's shuttered mines. An engineer and a computer programmer, they landed in the oil industry. This complicated work of logistics and data and fuel loads put gasoline in cars and buses and jet fuel on planes. Those white-collar 60+ hour weeks traveling and working on databases remotely that began when I was 10 remade my childhood into one of comfort while simultaneously imperiling my future.

Hand-drawn motifs of the combustion engine and dollar bills decorate these nesting dolls of coincidence. I crack open another matryoshka and my home becomes little more than timber and fuel locked inside one another. A different set of "little mother" dolls match this small microcosm of a home and a forest. The home doll fits inside the job market doll fits inside the industry doll fits inside the government subsidy doll. No matter how I stack these nesting dolls, there are some things I cannot escape. I cannot change that I was born in Big Oil's city Houston and not here, or that we moved so often as a family, or that my sense of security stems from their jobs.

Every time I come home I want to rewrite this personal narrative over and over, but I cannot leave out oil's gift of comfort and curse of change. I also cannot change that this place is the closest thing to home for me, or that hydrocarbons make up almost everything I touch on this trip. From the asphalt driveway, to the inner tube on the river, to the paddleboard, to the plastic badminton birdie, to the keys on the piano, petroleum is inescapable. The trees and grass too will become future oil, should they be submerged, subducted, and subjected to pressure. I cannot see a time when my future was not unraveling at the seams.

The light changes and interrupts me, turning the pages of my book all red. Smoke from the fires in Canada, or Washington, or Oregon, or

Idaho, or California, lofts over us. A moment of fear twists my heart and I pull out my phone to check InciWeb. I confirm there are no new fire starts in Montana and retreat inside. It is too hot and too smoky to be on the deck now.

Next to the window, safe inside from the smoke, C. sits at the piano. She has been practicing more new piano songs for two straight hours. Her feet rest on a stepstool and she sits on a pillow on the bench to keep her arms level. She chews her lip in concentration playing right hand melody first, then left hand melody, and finally chords with hands together. My partner tells us all, "She's already learned the first unit book in one weekend! She's so smart!"

C. repeats and repeats her songs as I read. Unfortunately for me, her favorite concert piece is Hot Cross Buns with two hands. As cute as this is, I can feel my nerves fraying. My joy at her newfound hobby mixes with a sense of grief. I worry that she only loves the piano because she cannot be outside. I forget that, unlike me, she has gained the beauty of a new experience. Music is mundane for me now.

The two of us clearly share some genetic code from my father's parents. Although we are a generation apart, C. and I both delight in music and playing games and being the center of attention. Separated by time and geography, we do not share the same baseline of what summer should be. I wonder if that will be a weight around her shoulders when she grows up and returns to her hometown. I wonder if she will miss a past she never knew.

In this hot and smoky world, I hope that this newfound love of music offers her solace as she grows. C. insists on creating beauty and joy in the midst of a changing world. I sense that wide-eyed sense of possibility and her natural curiosity will help her make a path forward. Her strong will reminds me of the famous Dostoevsky quote, "Beauty will save the world." I am not so sure that beauty will save us. My art has not hardened me for the fires. But for humanity, our creativity can help us find reasons to keep living in a world that needs saving.

Chased From Home

JO MORGAN SLOAN

SMOKE CREPT THROUGH OUR WINDOW at midnight that Sunday, beckoning the week with sinister acridity. The early autumn of 2017 was unseasonably warm and windy. Still, the threat was far beyond five miles to the northeast. Our quiet home in the suburbs could serve as safe haven to friends in the canyon if they needed it. Fire was frightening, especially with such strong winds, but it barely kissed Santa Rosa's air with its ashy remnants.

My small daughter, only eighteen months old, had long since dozed off down the hall. My husband rebelled against his own bedtime at the computer downstairs, reluctant to go to sleep simply because the October night was too hot in our bedroom. As the smell drifted across my nose, I had a fleeting thought:

If we needed to evacuate, what would I do?

I closed my eyes and saw the contents of our home in my mind: Upstairs, my husband and daughter. Downstairs, our four cats, two guinea pigs, and a fresh basket of folded laundry—not put away, of course, thanks to post-laundry laziness. Our legal paperwork was annoyingly well-organized in the den, a remnant of the good things my mother taught me. I could quickly toss papers into the basket of clothes and usher the cats into their carriers. The piggies were small enough to still use the cardboard box they came in. Maybe I'd risk grabbing one of my guitars. In two or three trips, everything irreplaceable could be packed in the car for a quick getaway.

The wholly fantastical scenario eased my mind, no matter how implausible; if by some strange act of God, the fire made it close enough to us to warrant evacuation, I now had a *plan*. I turned off the light and fell asleep to the woodsmoke that reminded me of napping in front of my family's stove in the Colorado mountains, where it was an unfortunate tradition to prepare for late summer forest fires. The faraway memories of black plumes on the horizon were a horror my new home could never achieve.

Our doorbell rang several times in a row, startling me and my husband awake. As if that wasn't enough, whoever pulsed the bell also pounded and yelled something unintelligible.

"Huh?" I pulled my phone close and squinted at the too-bright screen. Several missed messages and calls filled its face, all silent because of my Do Not Disturb settings. Three in the morning, and nearly everyone we knew locally had jumped on a text thread about the canyon inferno that was merely a bonfire when I fell asleep.

My husband Steve, who had evidently surrendered to the bed not long after I did, groggily stood to answer the door. I fumbled with my glasses and followed him into the hall to lean over the banister and asked, "Are we being evacuated?"

Steve opened the door, but our wakeup caller was gone. "I don't know," he yawned. "But the street's busy for some reason."

I peeked into my daughter's bedroom on the right. She hadn't stirred from the doorbell at all, but my husband was right—outside her window and to the south, our suburban street was filled with a line of red brake lights and bustling bodies.

What are they doing?

Steve was evidently too tired to find out and came back up the stairs, delirious and searching for his phone. "Did anyone text you?"

I returned to the bedroom and headed for our north-facing window. "Yeah. A slew of people said they were leaving a couple hours ago to be safe. I'm surprised your phone didn't go off if it's not on silent. But it wasn't close—" At that second, my heart slammed to the bottom of my gut.

The field beyond our neighborhood glowed orange. It was so surreal, so unexpected, that part of me wondered if I was still asleep. Black smoke billowed across the rooftops behind our home. It wasn't a kiss in the air anymore.

"Oh, my god—there's a fire *right there!*" I yanked my phone charger from the wall and scooped my laptop in my arms. The plan I'd made mere hours ago now guided my every move. *Laundry basket downstairs. Everything in the basket. The cats. The guinea pigs. Papers.*

Steve rubbed his eyes. "What did you say?" His lack of panic only made mine worse.

"Get the baby and meet me in the car. We're leaving. Right now." My instant alarm was good for one thing—clarity in crisis. If only I'd had half as much precision for minor inconveniences, my life would've proved much simpler to this point.

Did I even stop to use the bathroom before running downstairs? I can't remember. My movements were mechanical. A clock ticked in my mind, and no second could be wasted. The cats were mercifully all indoors and must've sensed the nearby danger, because they didn't protest in the slightest at being closed into their crates. The guinea pigs squeaked in conversation within their small box, answering my quiet mutters while gathering our paperwork. I piled everything into the laundry basket as intended, leaving the front door open while I took the first load to my car.

Not in Kansas anymore, I thought, amazed at how the sky could be so dark and so bright all at once. Unlike a Colorado snowstorm—where the streetlights would reflect off the low white clouds and give everything a wintery glow—the lights were all a threatening orange and red under billows of black and gray. Flames hadn't crossed the field to the west into our subdivision yet, but the wind blew our direction. The smoke wasn't an impressive tower miles from our home; we were within it.

On the street, an odd calm came over me, like the chaos hit a plateau and couldn't rise any higher. None of my many close neighbors were interested in asking or answering questions. They were far too focused on packing their families. For all that action movies played up evacuations with screaming and slamming car doors, it was frighteningly quiet. With the quiet came an inappropriate sense of safety, which was shared by a few people gathered at the nearby corner who watched the fire across the west field.

The threat was far enough away to bait my curiosity, and since Steve had yet to come downstairs, I crossed the street as well. We lined up against the fence, strangers who would now all have the same story. The flames roared with a low voice, beckoning all of our ears.

Within the drone... *Pop. Pop.* Random explosions. If they'd been closer, the sound might've deafened us. Every few seconds, *Pop*.

"What is that?" I muttered, expecting to be ignored.

"Propane tanks," someone said. His face has been lost to time and my fatigue. "I heard when the fire jumped the highway and took the K-Mart, the tanks in their camping section went off like bombs. Shot right into those houses over there."

"Incredible," I said. He might've been wrong about what happened to the K-Mart, but I had no reason to doubt his claim. After counting twenty pops within a couple of minutes, I returned home to finish packing the car.

The cats yowled in the back seat, and I ultimately chose to stuff my guitar in the trunk along with the laundry. The power flickered during my last pass through the house, making me grateful we parked on the street and not in our garage; if we did, could we open it without electricity? Privileges we took for granted any other time were now essentials that could mean life or death for all the people who couldn't escape.

Steve grabbed the baby and was only half-conscious when he came downstairs. I ushered him into the car and strapped our still-sleeping daughter in between our two cats. I blew a kiss to the house as we drove away, unsure if I'd ever see it again. We'd only lived there for about six months. It had never crossed my mind that our first home could be lost to something as absolute as wildfire.

The main street to the east was gridlocked. Everyone was heading south, toward the city's center. I turned north only because there was no point in hoping to get in the line. The other direction was free and clear—perhaps that should've been a warning in itself—but the black night and thick smoke turned the world into a different place. The local radio station was the best source of information, yet even they abandoned us; after about five minutes of airtime at 3:30 a.m., the disc jockey was ordered out of the studio by a yelling fireman. The station, like everything else, was on fire.

Out of the darkness, the hills were aglow. Beautiful horror, licking the tops of trees. We drove slowly and rubbernecked to the right, all us drivers hypnotized. False eyes of flame blinked from the skeletal remains of homes on the hill. Unreal.

Blue, red, and white lights forced us further north, and we couldn't turn west. The highway was closed in both directions. Soon, the way we came wasn't passable. Authorities shut down the southern route because of the traffic. People still needed our small street to escape. With no other options, we aimed east and guessed which roads to take. As long as it was *away* from the fire, that was good enough.

We found refuge in a church building the next town over, where we'd been directed by a few friends. One by one, cars arrived, carrying acquaintances in varying stages of dress as we'd all fled without warning. An unfortunate pajama party. Each of us had our own tales of woe, of panic, of how we woke up.

"Someone knocked on my door!"

"Someone rang my doorbell!"

"I smelled the smoke!"

"My mother called!"

Underneath it all, we all had the same questions: "Why didn't they warn us?" and "How could they, anyway?"

In the coming hours, reports were inconsistent. Most of us were certain there was nothing to return to. We shared videos online with anyone who would watch them and guessed the locations. Santa Rosa has never been a very big place, yet it seems many neighborhoods used the same blueprints, so most of us had several false alarms of recognition. After one's heart drops five or six times in vain, it no longer feels heavy. The carnage lost its power by becoming familiar.

The children were easily distracted with one another; later, those of us parents waxed on about how safe we felt to be together in a place where the kids could run and play without fear. It gave us a chance to do the uncomfortable—call our insurance carriers, our employers, our families from afar. Call our congresspeople to demand a working warning system. Find out what we'd need to start again, if we had to. Through all the unknown, nothing brought our community closer than crisis.

Once the sun was high that afternoon, drone footage showed the first real glimpse of damage. The neighborhood that popped across the field from our home, Coffey Park, was all but decimated. Every home we'd considered purchasing was leveled, except the one we bought. Miraculously, the flames stopped at the edge of the field on the other side, though we weren't allowed to go home quite yet. There was no power, no gas, and a high risk of looting. It was better to stay where we were.

From above, our town might as well have been Mars. It didn't take long for someone to juxtapose the drone images with Google maps to show the loss. Now the enemy had a name—the Tubbs Fire—which quickly became merely "The Fire" in shorthand. Millionaires and poverty-stricken folks were impacted alike, ultimately made equal through destruction. Our community wasn't entirely new to fire since we gathered supplies for towns further inland the previous year, but to that point, our fire was unprecedented. Never before had one burned so much so quickly, destroyed so many homes, or taken as many human lives.

Unfortunately for all, those titles wouldn't remain ours for long.

Despite the comfort of knowing that our home had survived, I itched to return and salvage anything that might've been damaged in the heavy smoke blanketing the area. In daylight, even though the fire still raged to the southwest, the danger was gone. Our suburb returned to the concrete safe haven we'd always presumed that it was. Sidewalks do not burn. What risk was a fire?

The local radio station was back on the air in the afternoon, ready to keep evacuees updated. Against all odds, the station had only been licked, leaving their satellites untouched. Those early days were essential for all, and no resource more important than our radio. They told us what was safe and where we could go. Broke the news of what landmarks were lost. What schools. When the main hospital would be open again. We were one by our ears.

The familiar, friendly attitude of the morning D.J. didn't match the unrecognizable city. Santa Rosa's charred remains were more appropriate for a funeral procession. On the streets of Coffey Park, homes were reduced to ghosts, eerily showing their heartbeats with still-flickering pilots on the natural gas lines. The metal frames of cars left behind fused to the street. Some I recognized well from the region's revered car shows—the black Model T from the collector on the corner, the Studebaker that once was a robin's egg blue—both reduced to twisting, ashy heaps. The white plastic fencing surrounding the horse pastures at the base of Fountaingrove Parkway normally looked perfectly pastoral, but they'd melted like candles and dripped tears of grayish white onto the grass. It didn't look like the forest fire remnants I'd seen in Colorado. This was a war zone. We had too many people, too many buildings, and too much solid infrastructure to be so easily wiped out.

In the wake of tragedy, communities unite. The people agree to be kind for a while and put up banners that say, "Thank You First Responders." They donate their clothes, their old toys, their books. Some even volunteer to help clean up the rubble. But something was lost that couldn't be purchased or provided by any outside agency or insurance claim: our sense of safety in our home had been stolen from us, stripped by the trauma of a pounding door in the middle of the night.

To their credit, the agencies that once relied on reverse-911 calls were forced to adapt in the age of cell phones. A new service, Nixle, became the ubiquitous answer to anyone's questions about local threats. While glitchy at first, it was widely adopted and remains the best safety net and resource for us residents.

"Did you get the Nixle about that?" we say, changing our language as was required.

Yet the issue at hand wasn't man-made at all; at least, not in the simplest form, like a phone call. Our whole world had changed, putting us at new risk. The following year, other fires came close, and if not, the smoke stained the world orange. Days on end were spent in an odd seasonal lull when the sun disappeared during cloudless days. School was cancelled for air, then cancelled for flood, then cancelled for lightning and wind. For never seeing a snow day in her life, my daughter has spent more time at home due to weather than I did my whole life.

As much as one might think The Tubbs Fire prepared our town for anything, history repeated itself two years later, almost to the day. The Kincade Fire, which began further north, resulted in a mass evacuation of the county which crept closer to our neighborhood in systematic waves. Instead of the stranger pounding on our door, we were kept awake all night by the gusty winds and screaming Nixle alerts. Policemen blared the special siren—Hi-Low Hi-Low—and raced through our neighborhood while shouting through the loudspeaker, "Get out, now!"

Tubbs and Kincade forced us away, and still, fires have raged again. The west edge of Santa Rosa burned once more amid the Covid days of 2020. One should not become familiar with fleeing into the night, though that's a skill all Santa Rosa citizens do well. The mechanical escape of packing to leave with our basket of laundry is a thing of the past. We now have a perpetually packed "Escape Suitcase," complete with extra pet supplies, a binder of our paperwork, and the photo albums we didn't think to grab the first time. Our pets have special quick-load crates, paper litter boxes, and collapsable bowls. All these options much better than how I collected our newest addition while escaping Kincade: without a box of her own, I put the pet bunny in a five gallon paint bucket!

All of this to say, it isn't the ideal of home that I long for. Not the cozy suburb of Northern California where we planted roots, watched it burn, then rebuilt. People are resilient. My daughter doesn't remember how she danced in the church halls for a week while we slept on the floor. She will only know the spooky Coffey Park car graveyard through pictures. Today, the homes that sprouted from the ashes have settled foundations and Nixle alerts have all but disappeared.

No—I long for something that can't be repaired. What's missing is clear air itself. It's been swallowed by the high heat of fall and a wind that provokes fear. In comfortable preparedness for near-certain tragedy, we sacrifice the chance to say that these days are firmly behind us. With our go-bags pre-packed, our assets in photographs, and Nixle at the ready, one must admit a lonely homesickness for safe Mother Earth.

Beauty in the Burn Scar

REBEKAH DOYLE

YOUNG AND FILLED WITH VISIONS of scenic alpine vistas, I backpacked through a heavily burned area in Montana's Anaconda Pintler Wilderness. Since the early 2000s, gradually, then suddenly, fires became a part of my wilderness trips, and then the flames burned closer to home. One June morning I was hiking along the Kachina trail in Flagstaff's San Francisco Peaks when I rounded a corner and saw smoke rising from the side of the mountain. The smoke expanded and I retreated to the trailhead as firefighters massed in the parking lot. By the time I was back in town a plume engulfed the peaks and my mom in Massachusetts heard about it on the news. Four years later, as a volunteer with Search and Rescue, I knocked on doors while ash rained in the Flagstaff neighborhoods closest to the fire that was moving up Oak Creek Canyon. The 15,000-acre Shultz Fire in 2010 and the 21,000-acre Slide Fire in 2014 were quaint in comparison to the smoke and destruction of the fires in British Columbia in 2015. We awoke to apocalyptic skies while on a sea kayaking trip in the Broughton Archipelago off Northern Vancouver Island. These and other experiences did not prepare me for seeing the mountains out my Tucson front door in flames in the summer of 2020 as 120,000 acres of the Santa Catalina Mountains burned for over a month. In August and September of the same year, smoke from California wildfires turned the Tucson skies brown, adding to the oppressive feeling of weeks of record-breaking triple digit heat. Friends and family along the West Coast experienced stretches of days where it hurt to breathe outside. In the midst of one of these smoke plumes I dared to hike on a mid-September Saturday. Deep in some of the forest patches, the air seemed fresh and I gratefully breathed in the reassuring scent of decaying autumn leaves. The open ridges smelled of campfire. It felt wrong to inhale particles of California grasslands and oak woodlands. I directed my focus to plants and insects close to the ground to shift my mind and breathing away from the troubling wider view.

Just as you start noticing a certain type of car when you begin driving that model, over the subsequent weeks and months, I noticed burn scars with increasing frequency. Fire is a part of the natural ecology of many landscapes in the Southwest. It was not surprising to find myself one late September hiking through patches of fiery aspen leaves glowing where there were once islands of pines in these high-altitude grasslands. The brilliant yellows, golds, and red-oranges also dotted nearby hills and more distant mountains, creating a longing to be immersed in these ephemeral colors. Groves of aspens that would not exist had the Wallow Fire not burned a half million acres in Eastern Arizona in 2011. Even if I had not recalled sitting at my kitchen table that summer listening to reports of the enormous fire engulfing Arizona's White Mountains, I had enough hints on this hike of what had happened as I stepped over fallen, charred pines interspersed among the dense young aspens and wove my way past standing dead trees, some mere trunks broken off halfway up, others a complete skeleton.

When I talk about how sad I feel about the intense changes happening to some of my favorite places and how this sadness extends to the children who will not know these places as I knew them in my lifetime, some have countered that they cannot miss what they did not know, that the loss will not feel as bad. I think back a couple of decades when I met a man at the Congaree Swamp–now National Monument–actively searching for an ivory-billed woodpecker after reports of sightings in the Southeast had ignited hopes that they might not be extinct after all. I stared at the posters that encouraged visitors to keep an eye out. I scanned the cypress trees and listened keenly while paddling the swamp and felt the strangeness of losing something that I never knew.

A twenty-something co-worker drove Tucson's Catalina Highway after the recent fires and said it was beautiful up there. She added that she did not notice much fire damage. She moved to town after the fire. Maybe this will become the new Instagrammable view: the burn scar. I have hiked in more than a few burn scars these last couple of years with renewed urgency to focus on the life in these transformed spaces. An ensemble of hairy woodpeckers tapping away at bare conifers and pines made it easy to see how forests of dead trees are still lively places. There is always something to look at. Masses of ladybugs on the rocks and trunks of scrubby oaks or lush tufts of grasses filling the opened spaces. But charred, flattened cacti in a Sonoran Desert canyon are less easy to accept. Saguaros are not fire adapted. Fires coupled with drought and extreme heat make it hard to craft an optimistic narrative of resilience. And yet, three springs after that intense fire in Tucson's Catalinas, I sat on a rock where a burned canyon met the ridge. The dead saguaros mostly absorbed into the earth, fresh scrub oak leaves sprouted from the bases of charred trunks and tangles of purple phacelia flowers blanketed the burn scar.

I spent my childhood in Riverside, Rhode Island, a small residential enclave of East Providence, itself a smaller version of Providence which seemed to be a smaller Boston in, of course, the smallest state in the union. Riverside was more urban than suburban in that you could walk to school, to the bakery, deli or pharmacy, to a relative's house and the neighborhood was varied in terms of the types of housing and the people that lived there. A drug dealer lived a few houses down next to a friendly retiree who had coiffed hair and gardened in meticulous outfits inspired by the set of a 1950s sitcom. A couple of abandoned-looking houses were each inhabited by an elderly woman that had probably been raised in the house and survived her family members. Our oversized grassy side yard graded into Miss Julia's weeds and bushes and walnut tree. Although I was afraid to retrieve a ball that strayed too close to her two-story brown house with several broken windows and no electricity to brighten them, there was nothing to be afraid of. She kept to herself, wore a plastic kerchief over her head when it rained, and a trench coat when walking to or from the bus stop. There were also beautiful homes with lovely gardens. Most people knew their neighbors, and kids like me played in the street and rode our bikes without an adult present by age 7 or 8. Despite the news about kidnapper vans and satanic cults, it was an easy, safe place to be a child, and I feel lucky to have had the experience of growing up in a culturally and economically mixed town where I was free to explore with other neighborhood kids.

I have long since left Rhode Island but the neighborhood overall seems a bit better than in the 1980s and the town has similarly aged well. The pond by the bakery and deli that we used to skate on in winter has fountains and park benches. The industrial decay that characterized the post mill-era Rhode Island of my youth has in many ways improved. Bike paths cover railway tracks and rivers once darkened by tunnels and pollution are bright and inviting. Waterfront parks are vibrant spaces. I ran along Narragansett Bay during a visit last year and saw an osprey circling overhead, a sight I never recalled from childhood. The pond does not freeze over with the depth and extent that it used to. There are many other markers of environmental change in my home town but I do not feel them the way I do when I am in the deserts and mountains of my adopted home in the West. I can conjure nostalgia for the Riverside of my youth, but little in the way of solastalgia. Perhaps this is due to the ubiquitous development and limited natural spaces that characterized my experience there than merely the consequence of time and physical distance. I learned to play golf at a municipal course adjacent to oil tanks, the air perfumed with petroleum. The small waterways that intersected the holes shined with the sheen of oil, which clung to the ball as you fished it out and wiped your greasy hands on your shorts. I formed a strong connection to bays and woods that coexisted with the industrial, and while trips to beaches and New England forests gave a taste of wild places, I learned to love what I knew and did not need nature to be pristine in order to appreciate it.

Perhaps it is how I experience Arizona's canyons, deserts, and mountains that deepens the hurt I feel when they are changed by fire. I do not own land or have a tie to a particular place that some people experience for decades or generations. As a hiker, biker, and camper I visit many places but quite a few are revisited and remain a part of me. A twelve-year-old truck camper feels like home in a way most residences have not. If I had the money for a cabin in the White Mountains, I'm not sure that I would want to settle in one place when I have had the luxury to know different elevations and habitats and see them change from season to season as though visiting old friends. Some campsites in the oaks of the Huachuca Mountains or among the aspen groves beneath the San Francisco Peaks are so familiar that when they are taken by someone else and I need to choose another site nearby I feel vaguely proprietary, irrationally offended.

I have been grappling with this tension to see the beauty in the burn scars while also holding space for the losses they represent. I am spending time in burned canyons, finding ways to feel at peace while also accepting that it is okay to not feel okay. Feeling nauseous when thinking about the plants and animals that did not escape the flames or lamenting soils hardened by heat and rendered impermeable to rain for months, if not years, is an understandable reaction. The swiftness and size of the burns and the massive environmental changes they reflect is an intense reality to accept. The climate catastrophe is driven by systemic forces. I cannot pretend that if we all drove less we could somehow avert the looming environmental disaster or bring back species already lost. The weight of accountability for climate change is overwhelming for an individual to carry or even to determine their share of the burden. Whether I contribute a little, or perhaps a lot more, carbon in my lifetime matters little now that the consequences of all those excess emissions fuels burns in some of my favorite places. The damage has been done and more is on the way—set in motion by the actions of the past and our lack of collective action in the present. Given these circumstances, how do I live now to be kinder to mine and other future selves? I think of the volunteers who plant baby saguaros and others that pull the invasive combustible buffelgrass filling the spaces between cacti and bushes on miles of desert slopes. I am inspired by Tucson's new FoodCycle program and the enthusiastic residents dropping off food scraps at various collection sites across the city. The food scraps are taken to a composting facility and the finished product is available to residents and community gardens. This pilot project shows how a shift in a system such as waste disposal can enable many people to make greener choices.

So many, for so long, have already been living with a climate so altered that it affects their ability to exist or have a future in the place they call home. Others seem to be accepting the new normal. I brace for a future of fewer forests and more burn scars. Of hikes in arid grasslands where trees once provided shade. I hold hope for the wildness these places will still contain, for a foraging black bear to surprise me with a huff from a thicket of chest-high aspens.

ECOSPHERE

The Atmosphere Between Us

ISAAC PEARLMAN

"We are paying with our lives for the carbon someone else emitted."
—Mohamed Nasheed, former President of the Maldives

ONE UNNATURALLY HOT SPRING DAY a few years ago, an old friend contacted me out of the blue. I say "friend" loosely; we had talked only a handful of times since high school and college twenty years ago. But my friend wasn't calling to catch up—he wanted to talk about climate change. Specifically, he was thinking of moving his family back to northern California near where we both grew up. Northern California, which in the last few years has been parched by drought, drenched by atmospheric rivers, and scarred by wildfire. My friend called me to ask if I thought moving back was a good idea.

I should be clear that I am not a climate expert by any means. I don't have a doctorate, I don't run climate models, nor do I publish scientific articles. I'm more of a science translator than a scientist. However, I have spent a good part of the last decade trying to interpret climate models, mostly for long-range planning purposes. Though I typically work anonymously behind agency and division directors, climate change has been at the forefront of my professional, and often personal, life for a long time.

Early in my climate career, it used to be when I told people my profession there often came a pause. Strangers would curiously or confusedly ask me *How bad is climate change going to be?* but then sometimes preemptively halt me: *Nah, I actually don't really want to know.* Grim humor in my liberal Californian bubble was common—*So should I look into buying some Oregon property?*—and thankfully skepticism wasn't. Although occasionally I have gotten into heated arguments with climate science deniers, including once at a friend's wedding, those were confrontations that I neither sought out nor escalated. People often sympathized with me about working in such a gloomy field, a bleak pity to which I usually volleyed back with my practiced dark humor about my personal benefit to our society's lack of action on climate change: *Job security for life!* Some just flat out asked me if we are doomed, to which my usual reply was *Well, only if we do nothing.*

However, now the tone has shifted. Most people I encounter these days don't seem to view climate change as a vaguely distant, bleakly humorous future. Now what my friend who called me and others want to know, with real apprehension, is: *Will it affect me?* Strangers have given me their home address, wanting to know about sea level rise, drought, and wildfire risk in their neighborhood, their school district, their town.

Without going into hyperbole, the unsatisfying answer to everyone is an unequivocal "yes"—albeit in a myriad of ways from barely visible to wrenchingly visceral. It may be starkly obvious like an evacuation from a hurricane or wildfire, huddling indoors with family during a heat wave or poor air quality days. Or it could be more subtle like a rise in the price of coffee or lumber or energy or water, just to cite a few of many, many examples. The reality is, no matter where you live or work, climate change has likely touched your life already. And as many in the fire-marred west, the flood-prone midwest, hurricane-vulnerable south, and sea level rise-slammed northeast know all too well, not all impacts are physical: the unnerving, low-level dread over looming climate change is a very real psychological anxiety that is now recognized with its own clinical diagnosis and licensed specialty.

From global supply chain disruption to extreme weather to mental health, the long-armed tentacles of climate change are squeezing us increasingly tighter. And yet after all these interactions with friends and strangers over the years, there are two things that stand out to me: first, that so many people who understand climate change is real don't seem to understand—or perhaps just don't want to believe—that *of course* they will be affected. The second, strangely enough, is that almost nobody wants to know who else other than themselves will be hit by climate change. Few people I talk to care to ask who the most vulnerable are.

My first exposure to those who will suffer climate change's worst lashes came in late 2005, when I arrived at a sleepy port town in northern Peru to start my job as a bright-eyed and bushy-tailed Peace Corps Volunteer. During my two long years in that arid, dusty coastal desert it rained only a handful of times; running water was sporadic and available only a few hours a day at best. The town, Puerto Malabrigo, relied economically on a dozen or so industrial fishmeal factories, which during production belched out black smoke and fetid brown wastewater whose rancid smell hung heavy over the town. The mostly foreign-owned factories processed millions of wriggling, silver anchoveta into hundreds of thousands of tons of pale powdery fishmeal every year.

But when the factories weren't in production there was plenty of time, as is so often the case in small towns, to sit around and share stories—which the citizens of Puerto Malabrigo had in abundance. Stories about the unprotected pre-Incan ruins just north of town, which according to rumors yielded local looters the occasional gold artifact to sell on the black market. Stories about the local whorehouse, which served industrial fishing outsiders in town for business. Stories about "Ceviche Mucho Bueno," an itinerant and constantly drunk gringo who came to town years ago and simply never left, earning his nickname via the only three Spanish words he spoke.

But above all, the stories that captivated me the most were about the 1998 El Niño. It is still today one of the strongest El Niños on human record, an extreme weather phenomenon whose global impacts ranged from drought in Indonesia to floods in Europe—and which temporarily raised the temperature of the entire planet by 1.5 degrees Celsius. The townspeople of Puerto Malabrigo told me the 1998 El Niño brought an immense deluge of rain to their desert, wiping out the only road into town. It was months before they were able to reconnect with neighboring towns and the district capitol, during which they were forced to start rationing food. My friend Nestor, an earnest and popular fisheries coordinator, told me the ocean heated up so much that fishermen were pulling fish out of their nets that they had never seen before, and had no idea if they were edible or not.

Even in good times, Puerto Malabrigo's ocean bounty did not lift all boats equally: high production meant more fishmeal export to North American, Europe, and Asia—mostly for rich people's pet food—while some people in town barely had enough to eat. When the factories weren't in production the town slowed, people cut back on spending, and the factories were shuttered and maintained with a skeleton crew. People asked each other on the street whether a ship was in town, as it meant a few jobs helping to load provisions and huge sacks of fishmeal, or if there was word when the factories were going to open again. Many young people left the town for the provincial capital to continue their education or to look for work. Financially, people had just enough to get by: enough to keep food on the table, to buy a family's first refrigerator, to slowly build or add on to their home one room at a time; leaving cement columns and naked iron rebar pointing up to the hope of future income to finish the addition. Life in Puerto Malabrigo was a steady, stable state that the 1998 El Niño pushed to the brink of collapse. And every year the odds increase—along with the earth's temperature—that an even stronger one will come.

In 1998 I was just sixteen years old and had never heard of El Niño. Though the small northern California town where I grew up experienced periodic heavy flooding, to me it just meant some free days off school. It wasn't until long after I left Peru that I began to connect the dots between greenhouse gas emissions from my home country, and extreme weather phenomena in places like Puerto Malabrigo.

By some accounts, climate change and extreme weather contributed to turning tens of millions of people into refugees in 2021 alone. This is in addition to the estimated nine million deaths per year caused by air pollution, as well as another five million or so deaths per year due to climate extremes as a result of all that air pollution. To put that in context, that's about twice the number of people COVID-19 has killed since the start of the pandemic—*every year*. These figures, mind-numbing as they are, are a result of warming our planet just a little over one degree Celsius. And current projections have us heating up Earth at least two to three times more than we already have.

And yet despite this, the world's top polluting country—which to be crystal clear is the United States of America (we emit less annually than China but we still almost lap them in terms of per capita and total historical emissions)—has utterly failed to pass any sort of meaningful greenhouse gas emission legislation. Although U.S. carbon tax or regulation would benefit all eight billion people on our planet (as well as countless future generations), it's spirit-crushing that our best congressional climate action in the last thirty years is the twice-watered down provisions that finally passed in the Inflation Reduction Act of 2022. The legislation, along with the Bipartisan Infrastructure Law, cements our national climate approach as an incentive-based one: we will reduce emissions by buying electric vehicles, retrofitting our houses, converting to wind and solar. All good things, but notable in that the heroic burden of reversing emissions falls upon citizens and not the polluting companies that have pushed us to the fragile climate point that we are at today.

But interestingly enough, despite the lack of political will by our elected leaders to actually curb climate change, there is a rare bipartisan willingness to pay to protect people from its impacts. Nineteen Republican senators voted for the infrastructure bill, which allocates billions of dollars for climate adaptation and resilience. This seeming inconsistency can perhaps be explained by the simple fact that the lion's share of pre- and post-disaster funding from the government has traditionally gone to wealthier communities that are better able to navigate bureaucracy to secure it, and not to the climate vulnerable people who need it the most.

An illustrative example can be found in California's Bay Area, where currently there is a multi-billion-dollar effort underway to shore up downtown San Francisco's seawall against sea level rise and earthquakes. The monumental twenty-year effort has already garnered hundreds of millions of dollars in federal, state, and local funding and is feverishly working to beat the next big one. The huge pot of predominantly public money will secure protection for San Francisco's downtown financial district which includes the national headquarters of Wells Fargo and BNP Paribas—two private companies which have made obscene profit by bankrolling oil and gas conglomerates. Meanwhile, across the bay in Oakland some of the most vulnerable and ignored frontline communities in California face catastrophic future flooding due to sea level rise. Yet there are no hundreds of millions of dollars promised for Oakland's crumbling infrastructure or low-lying shoreline dotted with legacy toxic industrial sites.

The overall moral gymnastics by our elected officials beggars belief: how they willingly shell out billions of our tax dollars to bail out our increasingly sinking ship, yet refuse to lift a finger to plug any of the leaks. The United States government lavishes over $700 billion on the military every year to maintain world peace—yet refuses to curb the carbon emissions that our own military intelligence shows can destabilize entire global regions. Instead, in 2017 our government spent about 100 times more on fossil fuel subsidies than it did on climate change.

This is how climate change goes from lightly touching us to putting half of the world's population (some 3-4 billion people) at significant risk from intense climate change, according to analysis by the world's top scientists in a recent Intergovernmental Panel on Climate Change report. And while that almost certainly includes impacts to me and you, it pales in consequence to what it means to others.

In 2019, with a master's degree and nearly a decade of climate work under my belt, I ended up in Panama working with a local university to assess sea level rise risk. Like Peru, stories abound in Panama about extreme weather events: the "La Purísima" 200-year storm in 2010 which delivered all of Panama's average annual rainfall in one enormous rain bomb, causing some 500 landslides and temporarily shutting down the canal for only the fourth time in history. A massive 19-foot Pacific tide in 2015 which flooded hundreds of homes and affected over a thousand "damnificados," or disaster survivors. When I first arrived in Panama in late August, the country was gripped by an unusual drought so intense that some cargo ships transiting the canal were forced to offload weight in order to make it through the receded water.

But the work with my Panamanian colleagues was trying to look ahead: how much could sea levels rise in Panama, and what would that look like? So on a hot and humid December day I found myself in a speck of a town called Cacique on Panama's gorgeous Caribbean coast, leading a dozen faculty and students to investigate how future sea level rise could impact the town's several hundred subsistence farmers and artisanal fishermen.

The first place we assessed was Cacique's simple seawall, which was basically a hundred foot-long chicken wire cage full of rocks. We measured up from the high tide line, and with a level to keep it straight we rolled out surveyor's tape to see where the new tide line will be when the ocean rises one meter, then two. By our measurement the ocean would rise enough to overtop the seawall by 2050, though in reality a storm took it out just months after we visited. Further down the shoreline, we found a low spot to measure once more. This time Michelle, a bright and bubbly third year marine science student, unfurled the stiff yellow tape as she walked past the school, the church, and crossed the dusty main street. "*Chuzo*," cursed one student softly, and another let out a long, low whistle. The 80-meter long survey tape reached its end before Michelle reached the spot in Cacique that is eight feet above sea level. Where Michelle stood, holding the tape's tail and blinking in the bright sun, was more than halfway into town.

The next month we did another field trip to collect data in Punta Chame, a small town atop a low sandy peninsula on the Pacific coast whose outlook appeared to be as dire as Cacique's, if not worse. Afterwards, I fired off a passionate email to fifty or so friends and family, railing at the injustice of how the developed worlds' lifestyle and emissions will completely upend life in these two rural Panamanian towns that are slated to get hammered by rising seas. A few people respond empathetically, supportively. Several point out what a downer my email is.

The majority didn't reply, and I don't really blame them. After all, Cacique and Punta Chame are just two tiny pinpricks on a global coastline of thousands of similarly vulnerable towns. Despite my attempt to connect them with stories and photos, the distance between the reality of these people on the frontlines and our own daily American lives of buying goods online, filling up at the gas station, and watching Netflix may as well be the distance from Earth to Pluto.

There is a scientific analysis which roughly estimates that the average American's lifetime emissions will result in the death or suffering of one to two future people due to climate change. I sit and think about that statistic often. Who will my emissions will harm–the children of my Peruvian friends? The students I worked with in Panama? The East Oakland community activists I've reported on, who have heroically thrown future climate change atop their present-day uphill battle against systematic racism and inequality?

It all makes me want to scream at the people I encounter in the United States who ask me about their individual climate risk, and then visibly withdraw from the issue once they see that their house is above projected sea level rise, or far from the wildfire risk zone. Would they care more if they heard how hard climate-fueled disasters have hit people across the world, and how it's a drop in the bucket compared to what lies ahead? Would they care more if they met a fisherman from Puerto Malabrigo, or a subsistence farmer in Cacique? If they knew the names and faces of those who stand to lose everything because of the United States' pollution and subsequent inaction?

After enough time in the climate field, it has become almost impossible for me to view anything the same because climate risks are everywhere. It's kind of like an augmented reality filter: this low-lying road I pass by by every day which already floods from today's high tide will be permanently under water in my lifetime. This nearby wetland with its graceful egrets, dabbling ducks, and carpets of pickleweed will likely be under water by 2050. This frequently flooded frontline community will probably not be able to recover from the next big one. A part of me wishes I could remove my climate filter, however there are just too many things that can't be unseen; whether it's the flood or fire projection maps, or the stark reality of the people I've met on the frontlines. I've started to make my old "if we do nothing" qualifier more insistent to folks I talk to–but in some cases, I simply leave it out altogether.

In the end, I told my friend that he shouldn't worry too much about moving back to northern California. Not because climate change won't affect the area–there is no question that it already is. But because unlike the majority of the Earth's population, he and the local government are wealthy enough to purchase more water supplies, make buildings fire-proof, raise levees, and weather climate change. The most vulnerable and exposed people, the people who I have met in Peru and Panama and Oakland and countless other places–the people who have contributed the least to climate change–will not be so lucky.

The New-Moon Bird

EILEEN MCLELLAN

I. NOSTALGIA

When I went to America, my parents sent me posters to decorate the walls of my city apartment. They were standard Tourist Board posters of the place where I grew up—County Durham, in the North of England. Flushed with the excitement of a new life in a new country, I looked at the posters and sighed. They seemed to me to be freighted with parental pleas: "Don't forget us!" and "Come home!" I couldn't look at them without feeling the weight of expectation, so I hid them away.

Over time, they have all been lost or discarded, except one. A dramatic photograph shows a dark, rocky hillside rising above a wildflower meadow, with a tidy, white-painted farm in the middle distance. The caption reads "North Pennines: England's Last Wilderness." The poster is faded now, that ghostly cyanic blue that comes from over-exposure to sunlight, with one ragged corner crudely patched.

What's missing is the soundtrack of the place, the haunting call of the Eurasian Curlew, *Numenius Arquata*. Both parts of the Latin name refer to its long, sickle-shaped bill; the curlew is the "new moon," "archer's bow" bird. The curlew's cry—especially the rising, bubbling call that it gives on its North Pennine nesting ground in Spring—is even more unearthly than its bill. The naturalist W. H. Hudson described the call as seeming to come from "some filmy being, half spirit and half bird," and in its combining of musical notes from the major and minor scales it speaks simultaneously of life and death, joy and sorrow, past and present. Listen to the curlew's call in one of the wild places it calls home, and you'll understand why it features in so much poetry, from the Old English (8th century) poem "The Seafarer" through W. B. Yeats to Ted Hughes.

For me, the curlew's call is a time portal. In an instant, I'm carried back to an April day in my childhood. I'm walking with my parents on Widdybank Fell in Teesdale, close to the highest point of the North Pennine chain. In memory, I see clouds scudding across a blue sky, sun followed by rain, rainbows sweeping across the rough grassland. I smell the wet wool of the Swaledale sheep, and delight in the curlews that patrol around us, defending their territory with loud *"Cur-lee! Cur-lee!"* calls. And I remember that my heart soared with the rising notes of the curlew, that seemed to say, "Here is wildness! Here is joy! Here is your heart's true home!"

Birds spoke to me back then. You might presume I was a lonely child, raised as I was without brothers or sisters, in a remote village, but with wild birds as my companions I felt part of a larger community that embraced me as soon as I stepped outdoors.

There was a dark shadow over this idyll. Far away in London, government decisions were made that would devastate County Durham and the rest of the north-east of England, that would close the coalmines, the shipyards and the steel mills, that would cause mass unemployment and destroy local communities. I escaped to college, and then to America, and assumed I would never look back.

II. HOMECOMING

The years passed by, marked by the typical events of adult life: first job, first house, marriage. To all outward appearances, I am permanently settled in America. But with each year that passes, I feel more and more drawn back to the landscapes of my childhood, visits becoming more pilgrimage than vacation.

A part of that pilgrimage was taking my dad's ashes to Widdybank Fell, the place where we had watched so many curlews together. As his ashes drifted downwards, I suddenly felt as if he was with me, dressed in the battered, many-pocketed grey jacket he always wore on our walks. He had a pair of binoculars hung around his neck, and—as always—he was laughing, at his happiest in wild places and in the company of wild birds. Even today, when I go to Widdybank, I sense his spirit there, mingling with the curlews for all eternity.

In my quest to understand the place I'm from and to which I always return, I've started learning more about curlews, and I'm devastated by news of their decline, with the possibility that they will become extinct in the next 30-50 years. I read of local extinctions across Ireland, Wales and lowland England, and fret for "my" curlews in their upland fastnesses. The list of potential culprits is long and disempowering: habitat loss, decline of food species, changes in agricultural practices, predation, climate change.

I read my local landscapes like a detective, searching for curlews, looking for clues to their future.

I come to learn the places they like. The high-elevation rough grassland, where Belted Galloway cattle graze; the heather moors, where red grouse explode out from under my feet with whirring wings and vexed calls of "Go-back! Go-back!" Places where the vegetation is of uneven height, providing shelter for flightless chicks. Places where the soil is moist, so those long curlew beaks can reach deep underground to find food. I make a mental map of places where I can reliably see and hear curlews; they are sojourns on my pilgrim's way.

Places like Dead Friar's Cairn, in Weardale. On a day in late June, the moor shows the first flush of the mauve glory that will spread across it as the pinky-purple bells of heather open to the summer sun. I have heard curlews here before. I walk along the trail, listening. Suddenly, ahead of me, I see one—no, two—no, three birds lift off from the heather. Even without the "Cur-lee!" cry, it's obvious that these are curlews: two adults, and a smaller bird that is a miniature copy of its parents. As they soar out over the valley, my heart fills with gladness. A curlew chick that has reached the stage of flight can more easily evade predators.

I try to believe that I will always find curlews.

III. DESOLATION

In 2023, that was no longer true.

I joined a group of other curlew enthusiasts at the new National Landscape Discovery Centre on Hadrian's Wall. The Royal Society for the Protection of Birds has identified this area as a priority site for curlew habitat restoration and community engagement. We watched a presentation about the work that has been done, including the construction of scrapes, wet areas that provide much-needed feeding sites. After reading some

THE NEW-MOON BIRD

curlew poetry and listening to recordings of curlew calls, we went outside to try to commune with the curlews and write our own curlew poem.

We sat for an hour or so in the hot sun, listening for curlews, looking across to fields where the birds were believed to be raising a family. I scribbled randomly in my notebook, hoping that some detail would provide inspiration for a poem. Every now and then someone would stare through the spotting scope at the bleached hillside where the curlews were supposed to be, willing them to appear, but the only thing that moved over the dried grass was heat shimmer. The poems that we wrote were full of sorrow.

It was easy enough to tell ourselves the curlews were still there, just out of sight and hearing. Perhaps, worn about by chick-care and heat, they were taking a siesta. Perhaps they had relocated to another, damper, field, where the ground was still soft enough for curlew beaks to probe for food. Perhaps—and nobody wanted to talk about this—they had lost their chicks to a fox, and, freed of the need to stay in the uplands, had moved towards their winter quarters on the coast.

Now, every time I hear a curlew, I stop and listen, afraid that it's the last one I'll hear.

Maybe, like the light from dying stars, their calls will still reach us after they're gone.

In June of this year, armed with my mental map of curlew locations and a new telephoto lens, I expected to photograph lots of curlews. I start with my now-familiar walk across Widdybank Fell. I know every curve of the track, every rise of the ground, I can pinpoint exactly where I've seen pairs of curlews in recent years.

They are not there. Lapwings divebomb me, trying to draw my attention away from their chicks crouched in the grass; skylarks ascend, their song becoming fainter and fainter as they disappear into the clouds; meadow pipits twitter on top of stone walls. Of curlews there is neither sight nor sound. I sit down, trying to shrink into the grass, to make my silhouette as unthreatening as possible. I wait for fifteen minutes, listening intently. Thirty minutes pass.

As the first raindrops patter down, I walk back to the car, defeated.

I'm wrestling my camera and backpack into the back of the car when a van pulls up. The two young men inside survey the binoculars, spotting scope, tripod and assorted other equipment that are spilling onto the ground. Reassured that I belong to their flock, one of them asks if I know where they can see black grouse. I'm puzzled by the question; I've seen black grouse here in the spring, but not at this time of year. After a bit, I explain that I'm looking for curlews, and ask if they've seen any. "Not a one," says the driver. "Not a curlew, not a golden plover, not even a bloody wheatear," he continues, naming common summer birds of the area. "We've seen nothing. The birds are gone."

Over the next few weeks, I go to all the other places where in past years I have seen curlews. I go on sunny days, on cloudy days, and in rain. I go in the early morning, the middle of the day, the late afternoon, the evening. I go to Dead Friar's Cairn five or six times. Nothing.

I think of all the other creatures that filled this landscape when I was a child, and now are close to vanishing. I think of the changes I've seen in America, the great flocks of red knots that used to gather in Delaware Bay each spring, reduced now to a few thousand birds; the bright waves of neotropical warblers that no longer fill the Mid-Atlantic forests in May. I grieve these losses as intensely as I grieve for my Dad—the man who stayed up all night trying to save the life of a sparrow, and who wept when it died. What would he make of the scale of wild death we now endure? The biologist E. O. Wilson coined the term "biophilia," meaning the innate pleasure we take in the presence of other organisms. What will we do when the last of our wild kin are gone and that pleasure lost? We will have entered what Wilson called "The Age of Loneliness."

IV. SOLACE

Greatham Creek, Teesside. Where the River Tees, which rises above Widdybank Fell, finally meets the sea. On this winter's day, the landscape is as leached of color as an old photograph, everything rendered in shades of grey: the leaden sky glowers, the creek water swirls in shades from ash to slate. The air tastes like iron, cold and sharp, appropriate for a place that forged the steel that built the British Empire. Across the creek, beyond a no-man's land of broken asphalt and high fences, industrial Teesside asserts its claim. In the foreground, the chimneys of a chemical manufacturing plant emit plumes of smoke. In the middle distance looms the Hartlepool nuclear power station.

A curlew, its buff and brown feathers the only hint of color in the vista, works its way along the muddy shores of the creek, its bill searching the dark ooze in search of food. It's most likely a winter visitor from

Scandinavia; our Pennine curlews migrate to Ireland. The bird seems not to care about the landscape, its attention focused on the mire and the rising tide, which minute by minute steals its way up the slippery banks. Soon it will be time for the curlew to leave the creek, to find a place to rest and preen and wait out the watery hours of high tide.

Here were once vast marshes whose grasses, at this time of year, would have been the colors of the curlew's feathers. It was the greatest expanse of intertidal habitat between the Scottish border and the Humber Estuary, supporting untold numbers of birds. Over 90% of this habitat was destroyed in the pursuit of progress. But times have changed, and now there is an emphasis on restoring what was lost, by rebuilding wetlands and recreating stream channels. Tidal flows once again bring food into the marshes for curlews and other birds to eat. Perhaps it's not too late to turn the tide for curlews.

I once got to hold a great treasure: the skull of a curlew, found on an Irish beach. Did it come from a Pennine curlew, possibly even from a bird I saw when it was alive? Do curlews think of themselves as birds of a certain place—a Pennine curlew, an Irish curlew, a Scandinavian curlew—or are they at home wherever they go? For years I would have told you that I was a woman of the world, as comfortable in Australia as America or Britain, but as I grow older I realize that I've always been a Pennine girl and the curlews will always call me home.

I gazed in awe at the sickle beak, picturing the thin sliver of bone tumbling among surf and boulders on the Atlantic shore, wondering how something so fragile could survive. Surely it symbolized hope—for curlews and for us—that the new-moon bird will rise again.

My First Love, an Orange Spring

ALLISON BARNETT

IT'S JUNIOR YEAR OF HIGH SCHOOL and I'm riding shotgun at what feels like the crack of dawn, 7AM, to get to the Antelope Valley, which is two hours away, to see a field of poppies. Most of our South Bay peers are spending this April 20th with a different plant in mind, but we had something grander to do. This year, the experts say the poppy blooms are unlike anything ever seen; they're calling it the Super Bloom. A once a decade phenomenon occurring after unusually wet winters, scientists are baffled at what makes this year the most super of all Super Blooms. In a time when news of unnatural natural events usually signals further destruction of the environment, this is a pleasant surprise. Accompanying me are two of my friends, Molly and Colt. Molly is hoping to get parts of her photography capstone done in the scenic flower fields. We drive through the rocky desert, whole lots of nothingness, until a small orange blossom appears every few feet along the side of the road. Now it's dozens. And now, it's field upon field of deep tangerine.

In the midst of these beautiful flowers, I'm texting this cute guy in my math class. He's a year older, he's the star of the football and soccer teams, and almost a star on the baseball team. He's got a big role in student government–the treasurer. He's a hot shot, and I'm pining for him. Everyone in school jokingly calls him "Big Game James." And somehow, I think he might like me too. One day, he sat closer to me in class, and every day he would inch a desk closer until we were now paired up for projects via proximity. I text him that the flower fields are stunning, and he says he wishes he could have come with me. I squeal as I show my friends. "Ugh, how about you guys date already?" they gripe.

I had never really appreciated the beauty of the poppy until now. Sometimes a few would spring up in the small plot of grass at my elementary school, and we were told by teachers never to touch them, that it was in fact illegal to pick them. I thought it was because they were the state flower, and then later got older and realized it must be because poppies make opium. And then, I got even older and learned, for one, elementary school kids are not making opium, and also, California poppies can't even be used to make opium. Contrary to popular belief, you can pick poppies all day long if you aren't in a state reserve. The teachers just understood how beautiful they were and didn't want us to ruin them.

Standing in the midst of a sea of tiger orange, my previous disdain for the color fades into deep fascination. Sure, there's the occasional lupine speckling the field with royal purple, my true favorite shade, or the goldfields adding yellow highlights as a contrast. But the poppy triumphs over them. Yet, they're still so delicate; there's a satiny feel to each thin petal. When the breeze hits, they ripple, a cascade of motion that makes the field look like an orange lake. This is being alive. This is good. I'm two weeks deep into being seventeen, I'm surrounded by nature's elegance, I'm with my close friends, and I might be getting somewhere with this guy. Yes, this is very good.

Molly takes out her camera every few feet and snaps photos of the scenery as well as a couple of us. I try to get all my best angles captured so that I can post something, maybe getting a like from him. Maybe even a comment if I'm really lucky and he's really bold. We step carefully over the sweet and fragile flowers to get deep within the blooms, finding pockets of dirt that are safe to step on.

Now James and I are almost celebrating our one year anniversary, just two weeks after my first visit to the valley. The newspapers and social media clickbait pages say the blooms are pretty this year, but not anything special like they had been. I want to go, see if he'll make good on his promise. The world has been stopped due to a pandemic, I'm not going to school anymore anyways. All I have is time and gas in the truck.

We make small talk all the way to Antelope Valley. We're saying nothing. God. It's just nothing.

"I wonder how packed it will be," he says absentmindedly.

"Maybe not a lot of people since they don't want to be in public. But maybe a lot because they want to get out and see something," I mutter back.

"Was it crowded when you went?"

"Decently."

"Huh. But that was last year."

"Yeah, that was last year."

Are we saying anything? Maybe we are.

See, James lost all that big game. He has dropped out of community college. He blows off all his friends. He's got a dead end job in a dead end beach town. Our date nights have gone from dinners at Disneyland and picnics on cliffs overlooking the ocean to hanging out in his room watching a movie. That's all we do. He's always high, which is ironic considering how low his life has gotten. And I should have seen it coming. I saw it on his graduation day. He turned to me in the middle of his party and said with fear in his eyes, "What do I do now?"

I'm about to go to college 2000 miles away. I'm trying to see my friends. I'm trying to make new ones. I'm working odd jobs so I have some spending money in the fall. I want to see everything. I want to do everything. I want to feel everything. And that's the difference: change excites me, but it frightens him.

This is the thing about the California poppy: it grows in the most inhospitable conditions, seeding itself as it pleases. It likes shallow, poorly watered soil. It likes to take root in impossibility, a stubborn wildflower that grows in the least expected places. But if you ever try to pick one, try to preserve it somehow, it will wither in your hands. The frail petals will drop immediately, and the forest green stem will curl into a brown memory in minutes. You cannot tame it. You cannot make it yours. You just have to accept where it has decided to spring up, and appreciate it where it has decided to grow.

Even then, the poppy will only last a few weeks in the ground. It comes around in the spring, and by mid-summer, it begins to wilt. The beauty of the poppy fields is not just in the sheer volume of flowers circling you; the beauty is really in its ephemerality.

MY FIRST LOVE, AN ORANGE SPRING

We park and find that we are far from the only people who want to immerse ourselves in the iconic flower fields. Sadly, there are many more dirt patches this year, and also, many other flowers. There are those tiny purple flowers, the lupines, begging for some attention, dwarfed in appreciation by the California poppy.

We take pictures, painting smiles on our faces. Or at least I am. We sit down in a dirt patch, people watching. There's a dog leaping in the field like a dolphin, emerging from time to time from the orange sea. James says he wishes I had brought my dog Biscuit so he could do the same. We laugh at the thought of my little mutt, who would probably cause great ecological damage if let loose in all this open space. We laugh, and I wonder if maybe I'm really smiling. Maybe I am happy.

Then the wind blows with a heavy hand, my hair whipping around my face uncontrollably. The poppies ripple in unison, but now it's a bother. Yes, the flowers are beautiful, but I can't even see with all the hair in the way. It was much more spectacular last year. I can't fight the annoyance. There's nothing left for us to do here.

When I went to the fields my junior year, I looked around, eyeing any potential snitches before I took a poppy. I just wanted one, but as I said, it *is* in fact illegal to pick one in this state park. I had a small vase of pressed flowers in my room, and it would be perfect. The first one I pulled was quickly lost to decay. I unceremoniously dropped it. But then, right before we left, I grabbed one more near the front tire, and put it in a small water bottle near the air conditioner. It would live, damn it.

Miraculously it did live, long enough to receive proper preservation. But it still is incredibly fragile, which most dried flowers are. This one though, I can't touch it without losing a piece of a leaf or having a petal flirt with falling off like a hangnail. It sits on my bookshelf, still a fairly vibrant orange despite its age.

I eye it now from time to time when I return home, a real smile creeping up on my face. I was an idiot to take it. It's lasted longer than I thought. Maybe I wasn't an idiot. Maybe I was a seventeen-year-old girl who liked pretty things knowing in the back of my mind that beauty doesn't last. Maybe the only way to preserve that is to dry it, to cut its life short rather than let it wither away in the summer heat. Maybe a token of faded spring days, cloaked in nostalgia, is better than trying to replant it somewhere else.

I don't think love is always a poppy field. I think sometimes it is.

Sometimes it is indeed a wily crop of flowers that lives for a short time, basking in the moment knowing it will one day return to shallow dry dirt. Some love is meant to be temporary.

That love I had then, that first love of mine, was a poppy field. They tell you the blooms are for a short while, that they are this fragile bunch of beauty that you cannot carry forever. And you don't want to believe them, you so achingly want to be as stubborn as the flowers. You want to say, "But see! See where it grew! It can withstand anything!" You pick out houses where you'll plant your endless sea of poppies. You've already named the kids that will play in the yard. But you're just kids yourselves. In your foolish state, you think you've tamed a wildflower.

You haven't. At least, we didn't. It's nothing bitter, and there's no "what ifs?" It was something to experience when it was there. It was something quite moving when blossoming. When it was the bloom of the century, it was all I had to talk about. I coated myself in orange, and then one day, I remembered it wasn't even my favorite color. Purple was. I remembered I didn't want to stay in California, much less my smoggy suburb of Los Angeles. I remembered I liked going out, I liked having all sorts of friends. I remembered I didn't even like watching soccer. I didn't want to peak in high school. I always wanted to be a little freer, to be my own person in this big wide world, and that meant I'd need to be on my own.

But he was the first guy to really appreciate me. He let me ramble on and on about pointless topics. Previously, the only dates I had been on were going to parties or just the precursor to see how fast the guy could get me alone. With him, initially at least, dates were mandatory to communicate how much he loved me; that he wanted to show me off, or show me a great place to eat, or just break up monotony. And even as our going out on dates began to stop, he never neglected me emotionally. I sobbed to him about what in retrospect was stupid drama, and he would always try to help me through it. He reassured me of my value and how much I meant to him constantly. He accepted that I was a prude; that I was waiting for something, and that something, I didn't know. He wanted to read my poems and little short stories, he asked to see my amateur paintings, and he always pushed me to chase my passions. Above all, he listened when I said we had problems.

And then, the problems changed from matters of miscommunication to matters of who we were. We drifted as we grew up. We grew into different people, and those people were not as cut out for each other as much as we tried to make the pieces fit. We tried compromises. We did try. But at least when we grew up, we grew wiser. Our fate was laid out before us, and we accepted defeat. We accepted that poppy season was over, eventually.

It's a week before move-in day for college. We're still stubborn. We're still dating. We don't really like each other anymore, but there's that tinge of love nonetheless. There's that pressed poppy of mine I stared at for an hour the night before that reminds me of it. But today is the last day. I put the last of my boxes in my truck. Biscuit is much more excited that James is here than for our upcoming road trip. We say all the cliché things you think you're supposed to say to the highschool sweetheart that doesn't work out. We kiss for the last time, and he tells me I'll do great things in college. And then he leaves.

My parents ask if there's anything left in my room that I might want, because they're sure as hell not mailing it to me. I look around, searching for one last memento to grab. There's a Polaroid of orange poppies with a few scattered purple flowers creeping into the image hanging on my wall. I snatch it off its clip and pocket it. I would find purple wildflowers, and one day even, I might find a perennial.

No Going Home Anymore

LAURA SELDNER

JUST BEYOND THE TREELINE the buildings have begun to rise, monoliths in the distance. Even in their skeletal form they already crowd out the blue sky, already this place is being swallowed whole. They will be luxury apartments, it's easy to tell from the wide windows and attached parking deck. Sitting in the park at the picnic table, I rearrange what's left of my sandwich–buffalo chicken cheesesteak, the same kind of sandwich I have ordered from the same place since I was ten years old– and nearby machinery thunders without mercy. The rumble of dump trucks, the scraping of backhoes, the voices of workers shouting to one another over the cacophony of metal and concrete. Ask and almost anyone will tell you this is the sound of progress.

Grover Park remains largely the same, down to the paint on the basketball court and the swings and the wooden bridge that spans the width of a bubbling, narrow brook. It is the same place I stumbled upon all those years ago when I had first returned to New Jersey, when I was a broken child from a broken family, the taste of loss fresh in my mouth. I force down another bite of my sandwich and wonder how long the tall trees whose shade I sat in, whose shade I sit in now, will stand until the machinery comes for them, too? How long will it be before this place is also devoured by the want for more?

When the tears begin to well in my eyes, treacherous and unruly, it is slightly infuriating; how much sorrow can one place hold? Ever since I left, I had told myself this place didn't mean anything to me; I was the kid who'd left as soon as I'd had a chance. Still I remember my eagerness to go and the way I disappeared, a ghost of my own making. Two weeks after high school graduation I threw everything I owned into garbage bags and piled them into a borrowed van; the only things I left behind were empty or broken, in a house that was empty and broken. Ever since, I had made it a point to mostly stay away from my hometown; around every corner was a memory, every inch of this place burdened with the weight of the life I once lived here.

The sandwich in front of me has turned soggy, drowned in too much sauce, disgustingly satisfying. My children have migrated to the swings and slides, their playful forms decades-later echoes of my own. And my husband sees it in my eyes, knowing me too well. *It's okay*, he says. And I don't want to admit it but I clench my teeth, sucking in the familiar dampness of New Jersey summer air, *It's just that*, I stammer in the fight to steady myself, *everything has changed now. And I have no one to remember this place with.*

There is a sanctity in the act of remembering, the way the mind can recall with such precision. The color of my mother's eyes or the way winter light makes a mirror of the snow. The first bike ride, the first tooth, the first day of school. The ugly curl of my father's lip when he spoke of my mother, all the unimaginable things he said. The sound of my father and brother screaming at each other late into the night, the same boiling blood running through their veins. The weight of my brother's fist against my back, the weight of his words in my ears. The smell of the earth after the rain and all the times I ventured into the woods and the way it feels to find a new place to love. The first kiss and every kiss after, the first love and every love after. The birth of my children, the first time I held them and every moment after. These are the things that ground us, the collections of memories that tie us to this earth.

The first memories I have are framed by the sun and sky of southern California, the place my parents moved our family to not long after I was born in New Jersey. We went so my father could chase his Hollywood-tainted dreams and it was there that my mother wrapped herself in a shroud of mourning for the life she once had. By the time I was six, our family had come undone, a supernova exploding into something destructive and blinding.

Our collapse was spectacular, the pain of it rippling down through the years, but still I dressed myself in the skin of a normal child. My parents' hatred was palpable, the air that surrounded them thick enough to slice with a pair of pruning shears, and still I went to Girl Scout meetings and did my homework and practiced Mary Had a Little Lamb on the piano. Time unspooled itself, Rumplestiltskin at the spinning wheel churning out endlessly golden California days, everything coming at a price. Unspeakable things lurked at the peripheries of our lives and whenever the tension became unbearable, wrapping its thick fingers around our throats, my mother and I would escape to the area behind our house if only for a few hours. It was a place that my six-year-old mind perceived as the vastest wild. And maybe it was, the way the picket fence of our backyard was the only thing separating us from what lay beyond; sloping hills sleeping like giants, red earth dotted with scrub brush and poppies, all the creatures that moved like phantoms skittering beneath the rocks.

When we walked our feet spoke for us, whispering back and forth in the language of displaced arid land. We'd search the landscape for cow skulls as white as the hot light of stars and rattlesnake skins discarded by their owners like ill-fitting clothing. I wanted to capture the howls of coyotes and preserve them in jars. I wanted to peel the silhouettes of bobcats from their distant perches and stick them on my bedroom wall. More than once my mother told me how all that wilderness might disappear, how one day they'd probably come and pave more streets and build more houses to look just like ours. Whenever she'd say it her voice became a melancholic, heavy thing. It felt apocalyptic to imagine; sun-bleached animal skeletons fossilizing beneath layers of asphalt, snakes having nowhere to undress, the wildflowers and cacti and yucca that grew there uprooted and shriveling in the southern California sun. All of it could be replaced with flower beds and manicured topiaries, our footsteps could be pulverized into oblivion. Those images manifested themselves in the hollows of my skull, vivid as nightmares, and I remember the night I sat halfway up the staircase of our house and cried, imagining all the ways things can change; the wilderness gone, my child body replaced with that of an adult, my mother dead.

Our house was sold, the inevitable conclusion for a family like mine. The only memory I possess of that event is truncated to seeing the realtor's "FOR SALE" sign in the front yard that was no longer mine, the rounded edge of my Converse sneakers making contact over and over again with the wooden post. After that there were so many places I lived in and left that by the time I turned nine I was ill with motion sickness from my perpetual movement. The one bedroom apartment, its walls as thin as wrapping paper, mold gnawing hungrily at the corners of the popcorn ceiling. The group home for every kind of child that has ever been forgotten, where we all buried our heads under our pillows at night, where we hoped tomorrow would be *the day* and it didn't matter what that meant as long as it meant we were leaving. My uncle's basement in Nebraska, my mother and I sleeping on the pull-out couch where every night I dreamed of tornados unraveling me at the seams. The small rented house across town from my uncle where the landlord always stood too close to my mother, always spoke too softly, always touched her arm too freely.

Nearly every time I moved I changed parents. Mother then father, mother then father. When I returned to the apartment in southern California and to my father, I became a haunted house, the ghosts of all the people and places I used to know dwelling within me. I went back to the school I had once gone to, but everything had changed. The house I had once lived in was no longer my house. Friends had become strangers, teachers had become eyes that watched me for signs of abnormality, everyone a potential witness to testify of my family's undoing.

When we left California we moved like thieves; quickly and quietly, my father driving and driving until long after the sun had set, until we crossed the state line, until he stopped compulsively checking the rearview mirror and he could sigh himself into unburden. My brother sat next to me and never let even the hems of our shorts graze one another; our parents were the only thing we'd ever had in common and I had emerged from the chaos of our family stranger and far more haunted than him. He didn't say a word to me until we reached Colorado, practice for later in our lives when we wouldn't speak to each other again.

After we reached my grandparents' house in New Jersey, I spent the rest of the summer avoiding my brother and trading one-liners from movies and sitcoms with my father, the only language we had in common because our mouths could take the shape of every word without ever having to say anything at all. I watched golden light filter through sycamore leaves as big as dinner plates, the whole world awash in so much green that my eyes became emeralds. I snuck to the rotary phone in the kitchen to call my mother and whisper into the receiver, telling her I missed her and our dog and the way the midwestern sky looked just before it would thunderstorm. I saw the massive skittish bodies of white tailed deer, how they froze in position then scattered when my grandfather banged on the window and yelled at them through the glass. I walked through the garage among the ceiling-high stacks of ancient National Geographic magazines and pretended they were the pillars of the Luxor Temple. I watched my grandparents fall asleep sitting up in their armchairs, then I'd become entranced by the enormous map pinned to the wood paneled walls of their den. I'd let my eyes trace every blue river, memorize which countries bordered one another, try to comprehend the vastness of the Pacific Ocean. And I'd create a mental list of every place I would see just as soon as I was old enough to leave.

Slowly I created my own map in my head; this new town, every dirt path, every pothole to avoid in the asphalt, every tree that lined the back of my grandparents' yard. Deciduous forests, a phenomenon previously unknown to me, became the setting for my own invented folklore. I traveled the faint and narrow paths that had been worn into the earth by the feet of others, relishing the fact that no one cared all that much about my life or what I did with it. I could imagine seeing myself from the kitchen window, my body moving deeper into the woods until it disappeared from view, until the forest clamped its dark mouth shut around me. I wove my way through bramble and every plant that I imagined could be poison ivy, my body a thread narrowly fitting through the eye of a needle. And on the other side of the woods lay the park, a place with swings and slides and a basketball court, a wooden bridge that spanned a talkative little brook; my childhood's dying breath.

When school started in the fall, I'd held on to the fantasy up until the very last moment; I was going to be the cool California kid. I had lived through *earthquakes*, I had been to *Disneyland*, I had learned to swim in the *Pacific Ocean*. But this town in New Jersey was not just any town, it was *the* town, and I was the foolish one that hadn't yet understood. It was the one with the Famous University and a colonial history and it was inhabited by people whose bank accounts had more digits than I'd ever thought possible. No one was impressed by California (they'd been there, or somewhere even farther), no one wanted to talk to me (they could recognize I was a lesser kid from the paper bag lunch and my thin-soled sneakers). I was never going to be the cool California kid; I had only returned to the town I was born in but it felt like I had jumped the subway turnstile and run onto the train, it felt like I had snuck into the movie theater without buying a ticket. I was tangled hair and dirty clothes, I was freak incarnate and haunted house.

Instead of having friends, I had places. I had the spaces between the library's tall shelves and the tree root ruptured sidewalk that bordered the cemetery and the university gate that sang like a choir when I held a stick up to the thick metal pickets and ran. I had the shopping center and its collection of never-visited shops surrounded by a mote of asphalt parking lot, all of it bordering my beloved Grover Park, the refuge on the other side of the woods behind my grandparents' house. The whole place felt like a ghost town which was the reason I loved it the most. No one would ask questions if I roamed the stores, if I walked laps beneath the awnings. I'd slow-crawl the aisles of the video store, staring at VHS covers and taking note of all the movies I wanted to see: *Jumanji, Clueless, Encino Man*, maybe even something that I knew would be drenched in swear words or blood like *Good Will Hunting* or *The Last of the Mohicans*. The stationary store reeked of Yankee Candles, possessed a holy grail level collection of Beanie Babies, and sold sticker sheets and even the kind dispensed from a coin vending machine, the holographic ones emblazoned with every 90's phrase I diligently worked into my vocabulary; *Whatever, As If, Talk to the Hand*. There was a grocery store and a Mexican restaurant and a pizza shop where I could watch through the window as they rolled the pizza cutter, swift and smooth, through the pies that came fresh from the oven.

By the time I reached high school and we had long since moved out of my grandparents' house, I had walked or biked nearly every street in that town. I had memorized the way each place looked in the extended light of summer, in the murky dusk of winter. My footprints and tire tracks littered the landscape; I had been everywhere and knew every place, I could navigate the town in my dreams. I'd head to town to the place that sold styrofoam containers of hot wings, or the shop with no tables where the guys behind the counter would shout *what you want on your sandwich?!* and I'd order a buffalo chicken cheesesteak. If I was feeling brave, I'd go to the store full of trinkets that always burned incense, the whole time the owner giving the stink eye to any unaccompanied minor who'd come in just to take up air. I'd go to the square where the kiosk sold newspapers and sodas, where the emo kids congregated on benches in their studded belts and heavy eyeliner, where the Mexican and Guatemalan immigrants sat up against the brick walls in their work clothes, their whole bodies vessels of exhaustion. I'd bike through the richest neighborhoods, pedaling sweaty and fast past their double-door entrances flanked with romanesque pillars, *I'm here*, the taunt I'd mutter between breaths, *catch me if you can*.

By the time I had packed away all my stuffed animals in boxes and plastered my bedroom walls with band posters, my mother's body had been eaten away, cancer performing its perverse magic trick of turning flesh and bone into tumor and rot. I hadn't known she was dying; the contact between us had whittled down to nothing, the venom my father poured into my ears was the only voice I had heard for years. Somewhere hundreds of miles from me she had tumors removed from her spine and she had to learn to walk again and still her skin and eyes yellowed to the color of bile. While she trickled into a slow death, I spent my time unaware, trying to figure out how to dress like the popular kids without having any money to spend and how long it would take for my boobs to finally grow and how to paint the fingernails on my right hand without smearing the nail polish.

On the day she died, my father told me I shouldn't bother going to her funeral and I believed him. Instead he told me to get in the car and we drove; the first and last time he had ever taken me to the beach. I sat in the sand and stared at the sloshing waters of the Atlantic and thought of the map pinned to the wall of my grandparents' house. I drew an imaginary line from my place in the sand to the other side of the ocean and whoever might be sitting on that beach, looking back at me.

For the first time in years I allowed myself to think of my mother, the midwestern twang of her voice, her fingernails perpetually chewed and jagged, the gurgling sound of her coffee maker, the silly quotes and pictures she taped to her refrigerator. I understood that I missed her and all the places I'd once lived, everywhere that had been lost to the past. The grief for my mother and every memory that died with her began to creep in and I understood that there was no going back. My mind returned to the wilderness behind the California house we once shared. It had once seemed unimaginable that my mother could die, that I could grow, that our home could not be our home, that the wild spaces we loved could become cul-de-sacs lined with mailboxes and bay windows.

I wondered if that place that we loved together had outlived her.

For the second time in my life, I borrowed the skin of a normal child. My mother's death turned me into a specimen to be studied by my father and brother, the way their eyes questioned me if I dared to speak of her. To them I was something curious, something strange and sick. But still the specter of my mother hung heavily over us all which was why it was the one thing we all silently agreed never to talk about. That September when school started up again and people inevitably asked *how was your summer?* I'd tell them too nonchalantly that my mother died and the pity on their faces was the only thing that reminded me there was grief to be had. But I did not know how to make space for grief so instead I found spaces for myself, places where my jagged form could fit in. There were plenty of forgotten corners in forgotten places, and my world became a collection of small sanctuaries.

There were only ever people like me in places like those; all of us a collection of haunted houses, all of us cut from the same cloth of struggle and movement and loss. Busboys and landscapers, cooks and waiters, kids who dropped out of high school because their families needed them to work, kids who dropped out of high school because they didn't have families. Everyone in that ivy-encrusted town looked through us, our lives made transparent in their eyes, but we could always see each other. I lived by word of mouth and my life became deserted parking lots and the alleyways between buildings. It was fire escape ladders and cars filled with cigarette smoke and the high school stairwell no one ever went down. It was the house that sold homemade tamales and the house that sold beer in the backyard on Friday and Saturday nights.

And my grief became a shapeshifter, a thing that lurked and waited and took any form but its own. Grief was a late night bike ride, it was perpetual music coming from my discman or the speakers of my 1991 stick shift Honda Civic. It was crushes on boys, it was wanting to be loved, it was the black and blue marks a boy who said he loved me left in places where no one would find them. Grief was a pack of Marlboro reds, a bottle of vodka stashed in my closet, it was sneaking into nightclubs and never knowing the name of anyone who danced with me. Grief was sitting by the side of the lake at dusk in December, wanting to leave town and never come back. And when I left, I did it without a single goodbye. I was pulled to other places: the urban landscapes of North New Jersey, the heat of Brazil, my husband's ancestral homeland of Ecuador, the state of Maryland previously unknown to me. Nearly two decades of roaming, the past and all its grief trailing behind me in my wake.

We can leave a place but never truly leave it. We can dream and move forward but we remain rooted, indelibly, to the places that have made us who we are. Time pulls us back, whether we like it or not. And it is then that we see how change comes in trickles, in steady streams, in tidal waves.

It started with my grandmother's death and the way our strange, disjointed family sorted through her things, their hearts seemingly unmoved. Her house was cleared top to bottom, a home ill with grief, vomiting a sea of boxes into the driveway, into the dumpster. I watched everything take leave; the record player and the avocado green typewriter and the ancient pillars of my Luxor Temple shredded to scrap. The maps peeled from the walls of the den, the tree in the front yard diced into wood chips, the house put on the market and quickly sold.

The stores began to change, one after another, snuffed out like candlelight. All of them replaced with newer, better businesses and if you asked anyone they'd tell you the place was made more beautiful because of it. The library's poorly lit shelves had been torn down and built back up again, every school I ever went to became a Frankenstein of constructions new and old.

Friends were deported, Immigration and Customs Enforcement knocking on their front doors in the early morning hours, grim reapers in uniform, the homes they once rented reborn in a flourish of gentrification. Those that weren't taken left, migrating like monarchs to friendlier climates, to wherever else might hold the possibility of home.

The hospital I was born in, the place where my mother–whose eye color becomes hazier in my memory with every passing year–gave me life, was dismantled by wrecking balls. Every place that was condemned for its lack of profit and utility, every parking lot and patch of unoccupied grass, metamorphosed into a multi-level luxury apartment building. Fields transformed into office space and university dorms, more apartments and more parking decks. There were no more alleyways, no more sunbaked fields, no more fire escape ladders. The forests grew smaller, the air no longer infused with the smell of decaying wood and damp moss and wet earth. Each time I returned, I only found a place that I recognized less and less.

When the pandemic plunged the world into chaos, I didn't return to New Jersey for nearly three years, to my hometown for nearly five. When I finally go back on a whim one sweltering Saturday in July, I know in my bones that this time it is real, now everything has changed.

After I buy our sandwiches (the guys don't shout over the counter anymore, now there are apps and screens and enough technology to ensure you never have to say a word to anyone) we drive to the shopping center, to the park that lies on its edge. I see the buildings in the distance and the machinery hacking away at the earth. *What the hell is this?* I say, the parking lot where I'd rollerbladed and made figure eights with my bike and learned to drive resting deep below the buildings that grow before my eyes.

It sounds bizarre, crazy even, to argue that an empty parking lot was important. Businessmen and landlords and architects and town councils will follow up swiftly after, explaining about property values and growth and innovation. How do you explain to someone that the parking lot, the house on the other side of town where a woman once sold tamales, the tall grass fields, the forest, are worth saving if they don't already know it?

I recognize this story, I've seen it before. How many times has my husband told me of his own hometown of Jersey City, how developers came and flushed everyone out when they realized it was a goldmine. They bought out renters and homeowners with pocket change, sums they would make back a hundred times over. Every immigrant family just like my husband's family moved out, every first generation kid whose parents had once been uprooted were being uprooted all over again. Everyone with nowhere else to go had no choice but to find somewhere else to go. The hospital my husband was born in also succumbed to the fate of becoming luxury apartments. All his favorite places were also converted, transformed, replaced, renovated.

I've seen this story before. What stood here in this place, in so many places, before someone else came along to claim it? The place I call my hometown was built on Lenape land, I am only a trespasser in this home. Beneath the asphalt and concrete is earth that was once someone else's home, every beloved tree and natural landmark demolished, a world made unrecognizable by the hands and guns of another. Every place I've ever walked is a graveyard where someone else's memories are buried.

Years after I'd left California, years after my mother had died, I found myself searching for the house I'd once live in. I still remembered the address, the numbers and letters ingrained in my brain. When I pulled up the images I could easily recognize the house, the paint still the same color but fresher, the same picket fence, the tree in the front yard now gone. Zooming out, my eyes transform into those of a bird and I see the world from above. Behind the house I lived in where once there was wilderness are rows and rows of houses, the streets reaching out long like greedy fingers. Our footprints have been buried, the snakes made to undress elsewhere, the coyotes howl from more distant hillsides, every creature with nowhere else to go forced to find somewhere else to go. From above the houses all look the same; like hungry mouths, like monoliths, like the black hole aftermath of an exploded supernova.

There is no *going home* anymore.

The closest thing I have to a childhood home was a little rented house I'll never set foot in again. All the friends I thought I had back in high school have vanished, the pull of their lives taking them elsewhere. My father and I do not speak to one another and I don't think we will ever speak again. If I saw my brother walking down the street I would not recognize his face. All the places I loved have changed or been torn down and built anew. This town is an echo, it is the shadow of a phantasmic form. I'd not thought it possible to stand in one place and miss it all at once. This place is my home but it will also never be my home again. And there is no one to share these things I carry with, no one I know anymore who also comes from the same place I do. There is nothing I can do but watch all my small sanctuaries disappear into the dark mouth of the future, insatiable in its want for more.

When I think of this town, I still remember it as it was and not as it is. And I want to think that places remember us, too. That the land recalls through its long and unfaltering memory the weight of those who set foot there. If it does, I hope it thinks of me kindly. I hope the land knows I found solace in every inch of forest, every field, every dirt path, every night under its blanket of stars. And I hope the land knows it was loved.

I have some recurring dreams—teeth falling from my mouth in a pearlescent rain, the inability to remember an important phone number, the panic of not being able to get into my middle school locker. But in one particular dream I am in front of my grandparents' house, biking down the street. The slope is steeper than I remember and I'm practically flying. I always think I am going to the park, that I'll make a right and turn onto the gravel path that leads to the swings and slides and small brook. But instead I am carried forward, pedaling up along the street past all the houses until things become strange and distorted in the way of dreams. That is when I understand; this place is unfamiliar and I don't know where I'm going.

About the Contributors

ALLISON BARNETT is a Los Angeles-raised quasi-Southerner, the daughter of two almost lifelong Mississippians who decided to raise their daughter in a concrete jungle. She has been published in *Cowboy Jamboree* and *Anchora*. As a graduate from the University of Mississippi, she has received multiple writing awards including the Barry and Susan Hannah Award. In her spare time, she hopes to create world peace, or at least her own peace.

CAITLIN CACCIATORE is a queer poet, writer, and essayist based on the outskirts of New York City. She believes that literature has the power to change minds and start movements. Her work has appeared in *Bacopa Literary Review*, *Sylvia Magazine*, and *Sunlight Press*, among other literary magazines, journals, and anthologies.

REBEKAH DOYLE is a physical therapist and educator who enjoys exploring the Borderlands and beyond by foot, pedal and paddle. She is grateful to live with her biologist husband in Tucson where good food and varied conversation with friends happens often and outside. She is a contributor to *Arizona Spotlight* on Arizona Public Media. More of her writing can be found at rebekahdoyle.com

CAROLYN JONES is a freelance reporter covering climate and environment stories. She's working on a novel about climate change as well as a series of non-fiction essays about the environment. She can be found at www.carolynjoneswrites.com.

ABOUT THE CONTRIBUTORS

KYRA MATHEWS is an Associate Creative Director crafting narratives and brand identities for global giants like Nestlé and The Louvre. With an M.A. in Creative Writing & Publishing, her work explores themes of identity politics, culture, and food, often appearing in varied corners of the Internet. She is currently working on "I Speak Brown," a website that combines storytelling and history, shedding light on how India helped shape the English language in unknown ways. Originally from Mumbai, India, she currently lives in Dubai, UAE.

EILEEN MCLELLAN is a writer, scientist and naturalist who lives and works in England and the U.S. With over 25 years' experience at the interface of environmental science and policy, her work has been published in scientific journals, trade periodicals and community magazines. As a volunteer with nature organizations in both the U.S. and the U.K., she frequently lectures and leads field trips on natural history. She splits her time between the mid-Atlantic states and the North of England.

ISAAC PEARLMAN has worked in the climate resilience and adaptation field for over a decade, both internationally and in his home state of California. You can find more of his writing in *KneeDeep Times*, *Sierra Magazine*, the *San Francisco Estuary News Magazine*, or at isaacpearlman.wordpress.com.

A freelance writer and editor, **MONISHA RAMAN'S** essays have been published by *New Asian Writing, Inquisitive Eater-New School Food, Kitaab, Where the Leaves Fall, Impermanent Earth, Terralingua Langscape, The Curious Reader, Spacebar Magazine, The Punch Magazine, SustainabilityNext, Planted Journal, Purple Pencil Project and Feminism* in India. Her works of fiction have been published by *Borderless Journal, Usawa Literary Review, Phenomenal Literature GJLL, Bengaluru Review, The Punch Magazine, Active Muse, Indian Ruminations, Asian Extracts, The Universe Journal,* and *Storizen Magazine*. Her work was a part of the anthology Narratives in Domestic Violence by the International Human Rights Arts Movement. She is an alumnus of Granta Writers' Workshop (nature writing). Her debut work is forthcoming with the Running Wild Press. She lives in Chennai, South India and is currently studying indigenous perspectives in conservation.

ABOUT THE CONTRIBUTORS

CLAIRE ROBERTSON-PREIS is a writer and singer living in Portland, OR. Her childhood was split between Montana and Texas, where she spent many hours on horseback and in the theater. Her professional work performing and creating immersive music experiences explores the connection between creativity and environmental justice.

R. D. SALMON is a single parent of three and a former nurse with a special interest in palliative care. Having lived for many years on the coast of west Wales, she now lives and works in Shrewsbury, Shropshire, being self-employed as a massage therapist and hypnotherapist. She has had a variety of articles published ranging from social history to hypnotherapy, has had poetry published in anthologies and recently self-published her first novel, *Haunted: Letters from Elspeth*.

LAURA SELDNER is an emerging writer of fiction, creative nonfiction, and poetry. Originally from New Jersey, she is a graduate of Rutgers University. Her work has been published in *Nonprofit Quarterly*, *No Tokens*, *Dark Mountain*, and elsewhere, and was nominated for Best of the Net in 2022.

JO MORGAN SLOAN is an audiologist, an artist, and a novelist in Northern California. Their debut novel will be released by Midnight Meadows Publishing in December 2024 with a second unrelated novel in July 2025. Jo's essay work can also be found in online periodical *Drunk Monkeys*.

MARIE WINFIELD writes about all things cities, transitions and memory at *Peripatetic Dreams* (winfieldmm.substack.com). She is from New York City and currently based in Berlin. Her legal background in fair housing and work in community planning drives her interest in how urban communities across the globe develop. Previously, she contributed a non-fiction anthology on bus travel, *Get on the Bus*, and is currently working on an essay collection on Black hair and a project about Black prisoners in the Ruhleben internment camp in Berlin.

About the Guest Judge

ERICA HOFFMEISTER is a rambling soul from Southern California who currently lives in Denver where she teaches creative writing and rhetoric. She is the author of three hybrid poetry collections: *Lived in Bars* (Stubborn Mule Press, 2019), *Roots Grew Wild* (Kingdoms in the Wild Press, 2019), and *All the Parts You Haven't Lost* (ELJ Editions, 2024) and considers herself a cross-genre writer with a variety of short fiction, creative nonfiction, poetry, and critical articles published. She's obsessed with pop culture, cross country road trips, and her two daughters, Scout and Lux.

www.ingramcontent.com/pod-product-compliance
Lightning Source LLC
Chambersburg PA
CBHW070202100426
42743CB00013B/3010